AF333668

ENLIGHTENMENT

The Key to Survival in
the 21st Century

FranCelia Woodward

Library of Congress Catalog 99-73190
ISBN 1-58151-054-3

Cover Design by Richard Ferguson
Text Design by Kathie Clark-Lauer

BookPartners, Inc.
P.O. Box 922
Wilsonville, Oregon 97070

Dedication

This book is dedicated to you
who are seeking enlightenment.
When you achieve your goal,
you will receive the crown of righteousness.
Cosmic Truth will then be yours —
the Truth that will set you free.

With love,

FranCelia

Table of Contents

Preface

Ancient and modern seers have predicted that great Earth changes will occur between now and the year 2012. There will be an increase in the number and intensity of earthquakes, volcanic eruptions, typhoons, hurricanes, and other natural disasters. Many will not survive these catastrophes. So you may ask, "Just exactly what is enlightenment, and how can achieving it help me to survive in the 21st century?"

Enlightenment is the expanding of our consciousness beyond the limited physical plane. It is a personal experience through which we are able to transcend our minds and bodies and attain a sense of unity and continuity with the Infinite. When we have achieved enlightenment, we will be able to view these disasters not with fear and dread, but with faith and understanding. We will be aware that all of these occurrences are a necessary part of Earth's transition into the 21st century.

To help us reach our goal of enlightenment, we each have a personal counselor who is always available to give us advice and encouragement. Our counselor knows us better than we know ourselves. This personal counselor is our Higher Self. Other names for the Higher Self are Guardian Angel, Holy Spirit, Heavenly Father, and Twin Soul. We would probably not be able to attain enlightenment without the help and guidance of our Higher Self.

As we become more aware of who we truly are, we will begin to realize that we are multidimensional beings. Besides the physical body, we have an energy (etheric) body, an emotional (astral) body, and a soul (spiritual) body. Each of our bodies is important to our whole being. Now is the time for us to learn how to control our minds and emotions and bring all our bodies into perfect harmony and alignment to prepare us for enlightenment.

There is really nothing we have to do first to reach enlightenment, because we already have within us all the potential that we need. The actual experience is not a sequential process, nor is it a complicated ritual. It can occur in an instant when everything becomes crystal clear. However, most of us will probably work our way gradually toward enlightenment. It is not an experience for just the privileged few: it is within the reach of each and every one of us. When it does take place, it will be as easy as breathing. We will just know the Truth!

There is nothing that can keep us from achieving our goal of enlightenment except ourselves. We don't need to have any particular experience or virtue. We don't even need to be perfect. Enlightenment is a direct, personal experience of a sense of oneness with all humanity. It is the peace that passeth understanding. It is cosmic consciousness!

— FranCelia

ENLIGHTENMENT

The Key to Survival in
the 21st Century

1

Adjusting to Our
Physical Transformation

Physical

What an exciting time to be living here on Earth! We have reached the end of an Earth cycle that began when humans first inhabited this planet. Some have called this the end of the world. In a way, it will be the end of Earth as we know her. Everything in physical form at this time will experience something that has never happened before in the history of planet Earth. Earth is being transformed from the third to the fourth dimension. As the frequency, or the rate at which molecules vibrate, is increased, every atom and molecule will be affected. This change will affect not only us on an individual level; it will also affect all plants and animals on our planet. The only way to survive is to adjust physically to the increased vibrational field of energy we are about to enter. The plants, animals, and humans who are unable to adjust to the higher frequencies will be left behind. We who are raising our vibrations will become citizens of the fourth-dimensional Earth, filled with light and love.

Within our lifetime, more changes are taking place in the human body than have occurred in the total of all previous lifetimes. In the next few years, many of us will experience tremendous physical as well as emotional changes. It is important that we recognize and learn to adapt to these changes which are taking place within our bodies. Because we are all unique, the physical and emotional symptoms will differ from person to person as our bodies are being prepared to withstand the higher frequencies. When these changes begin and when they are completed depend on each individual and their level of openness and acceptance of the fact that this cellular transformation is necessary if we are to make our evolutionary leap into the fourth dimension.

The process of transforming our bodies from the vibrations of the third to the fourth dimension is being accelerated at a tremendous pace so that we will be prepared to handle the incoming energies. As the electromagnetic energy is increased and we absorb these transforming rays, we will feel their effects more and more. As each cell of our body becomes more energized, our blood pressure and body temperature may become lower than what is considered to be normal. We may also notice that the aging process, which seems to be happening quite rapidly to some people, will start to slow down and become stabilized. As the cosmic energies flow throughout our body, they will bring healing and regeneration to our cells.

The changes and adjustments to our body are being carefully orchestrated by our Higher Self. These changes are occurring because our DNA, which is our personal blueprint, is being reprogrammed. Our cells are being transformed to prepare them for the higher electromagnetic energy. The cellular information that has been encoded into the DNA of our body is now being activated.

The cell is the basic unit of all life. Most cells are so small that they can be seen only under a microscope. A cell is alive. It breathes, takes in food, and gets rid of waste. It grows and reproduces, and in time it dies. Biologists are working on the theory that each cell contains a program telling it how many times it is allowed to divide. When that limit is reached, the physical body starts to decline. Most cells reproduce by dividing, so that there are two cells where there once was one. When a cell divides, each of the two new cells gets a copy of the master plan. This master plan is a chemical substance called DNA. The unique DNA code makes every living thing different from all other living things.

Until a few years ago, we were relatively unaware of the way the DNA could be altered. As scientists learn more about DNA and the genetic code, they may be able, by altering the code, to eliminate hundreds of inherited physical and mental defects. Scientists may also be able to control cancer and other diseases that arise in the cell. They may even be able to replace worn-out or diseased tissues and regrow amputated limbs. They may also be able to alter the DNA to slow down the aging process and increase the lifespan.

If the scientists on Earth have achieved the ability to alter our DNA, then it should come as no surprise to us that the Higher Beings are also able to bring about changes in our body by reprogramming our DNA. Planetary life is being prepared for the dimensional shift from the third to the fourth dimension through this cellular transformation process. Our DNA was genetically designed to be activated to accommodate these higher vibrations. The blueprint for the work we have chosen to do is also encoded in our DNA. We don't have to be given instructions by someone outside ourselves. Our Higher Self has all the answers. It's time for us to become aware of our own importance as a vital part of the coming age.

As our vibrations are raised, we will experience an increased sensitivity to sounds, smells, and the environment around us. Our range of hearing will expand and we will be able to hear sounds that were inaudible before. We will also become more sensitive to noise. We may experience a ringing or buzzing in one or the other ear for a short time as our hearing is being adjusted. Our physical sight will also need to be adjusted as it interacts with the opening of our third eye. As these changes are being made, we may experience spots before one or the other eye for a short time. My Higher Self explained that we need to relax and rest as these important adjustments to our ears and eyes are being made. The discomfort will last only a short while, and it is a necessary part of our transformation. (If the discomfort continues over a long period, it is important to get medical advice.)

Although our physical body does age, the rate at which this process occurs varies from person to person. As our DNA is reprogrammed and our vibrations are raised, we can live to be eighty-five or ninety and beyond and still be mentally, emotionally, and physically healthy. When our life is filled with positive emotions and thoughts, we can have as much energy and enthusiasm as people ten or fifteen years younger. Even though aging is a natural process that can't be stopped, it can be slowed by a healthy lifestyle. However, even in the best of circumstances, most of our vital functions do deteriorate with age. Our physical body is composed of substances that can be used only in the physical world. This built-in obsolescence is intended to make it easier for us to let go of the physical body, through death, when it's time to move our consciousness into the higher-dimensional body.

As our bodies are being transformed, we may experience a combination of new aches and pains in various parts of our body. We may also experience a gain in weight due to our body's decreasing need for food. Skin problems, such as eczema and psoriasis, often indicate that the body is cleansing itself from the inside outward. Our central nervous system will be affected because it will need to be *rewired* to enable it to handle the increased electrical energies. We may experience headaches or sudden pain in the head or eyes. For several days, I was feeling a reoccurring, sharp pain in the right side of the back of my head. The pain lasted only a short while, but I was concerned about it. When I mentioned my distress to a close spiritual friend, she said that she had experienced a similar pain. Her Higher Self had told her that it was the result of some necessary *rewiring*. In all cases, we need discernment to know if medical attention is necessary for any of our aches or pains.

Last year, several times a month, I'd wake up feeling dizzy. Even as I was lying in bed, a wave of dizziness would come over me, leaving me feeling disoriented for a few minutes. My Higher Self told me not to be concerned over an occasional bout of dizziness of short duration because this is a natural response as our bodies are being cleansed of all residual negativity in preparation for the incoming higher vibrations. Dizziness, headaches, and other discomforts are all part of the transformation our bodies may experience.

Physical problems such as fluid accumulation in the

inner ear may also cause dizziness. Certain emotional disorders — such as depression, anxiety, and panic attacks — are also common causes of chronic dizziness. When dizziness occurs frequently or doesn't go away at all, we need to get professional help to discover the cause. After a head injury, or when there is diminished hearing, prompt medical attention is necessary.

Not all of the symptoms that we may experience as our vibrations are being raised will be connected to the physical body. Other symptoms are related to the energy body, which interpenetrates the physical body and extends about an inch beyond it. This colorless body is connected to the physical body by a short cord at the navel area, and the two remain joined together for life. Because our energy body acts as a receiver for the electromagnetic energies, it needs to be prepared to accommodate the incoming higher vibrations. The most common symptom that accompanies these changes is exhaustion. We are used to physical activity making us tired, but now internal activity, of which we are probably not aware, can also leave us exhausted. This tiredness is a signal that we need more rest and sleep as the cells of our body are being restructured.

As our vibrations are being raised, symptoms may also occur in our emotional body, which interpenetrates both the physical and energy bodies and extends several inches farther. The emotional body is connected to the physical body at the solar plexus area by a cord that is extremely long and elastic. As changes occur in our emotional body, we may experience moments of great joy which are followed, for no apparent reason, by depression. We may feel more anxious or irritable, as if we are out of sync with ourselves and the people around us. We may become restless and begin to realize that our attention span is becoming shorter and shorter. At times, we may feel as if our old life is dying and we are waiting impatiently for a new life to emerge.

During this time of transition, the best advice we can follow is to be kind to ourselves. The more we resist the changes that are occurring, the more painful they may seem. It will be easier for us if we are able to accept these experiences with a positive attitude.

According to the Higher Beings, our third-dimensional world is currently vibrating at a frequency of about 3.5. The vibration will continue to increase until it becomes 4.0, and at that time we will have made the transition from the third to the fourth dimension. It's not just our planet, however, but our whole solar system that is evolving. All the other planets in our solar system are already vibrating at the fourth level or above. Each will evolve upward to a higher frequency. At long last, Earth will have finally moved into the fourth dimension.

If it has taken Earth billions of years to reach only halfway to the vibrations of the fourth dimension, how long will it take to make it the rest of the way? In the next few years, we are going to receive a tremendous energy boost. We have been told by the Higher Ones that our solar system is preparing to enter a vast region called the Photon Belt. This has been described as a huge mass of light and highly charged energy which will transform our whole solar system. As our solar system enters the Photon Belt, there will be greater spiritual light and love for us to assimilate. This will affect every cell in all the plants, animals, and humans on Earth. It will give Earth and its inhabitants the boost they need to become transformed into the vibrations of the fourth dimension.

As our solar system enters the Photon Belt, the two worlds of consciousness will become even more obvious:

the world of negativity, including fear and hate, versus the world of love and life. Eventually, those who adhere to the negative world will no longer be welcome on our planet. We who are striving for enlightenment will experience an identity shift as we realize that we are more than just physical beings — that we are, indeed, the spirit of life and love itself.

Obviously, not all of the pain, discomfort, and illnesses that we may be experiencing can be attributed to the transformation taking place in our bodies at this time. Some of our physical problems may be the result of our energy body being depleted. Still other illnesses may be caused by our thoughts or by negative emotions that we may be harboring. Doctors now know, for example, that certain substances produced by the brain transform thoughts and emotions into chemicals, and that these chemicals in turn affect the physical body, either positively or negatively.

There is now evidence that the mind, body, brain, and immune system are not separate but work together. More and more doctors have discovered that there is no disease of any kind that is entirely physical in nature, and there is no disease that is entirely mental. Even though the symptoms may seem to be only physical, the mind-body connection occurs in all illness. Since this is true, it is necessary to treat the whole person in order to achieve complete healing of any illness. The whole person includes body, mind, and emotions. If any one of these parts is out of tune, it can affect the other parts.

The pituitary is the master gland of the endocrine system. Our thoughts and emotions affect this gland and stimulate the flow of hormones, the chemical compounds that influence the cells of our body. Our body has its own healing system, a pharmacy that makes natural drugs to counteract illness. Peaceful thoughts release peaceful hormones such as cortisone, which is a tissue tranquilizer. A person under great stress or rage is interfering with his own internal pharmacy. Angry or fearful thoughts release aggressive hormones such as adrenaline, which signals a fight-or-flight reaction.

Thoughts of helplessness and defeat impede the flow of air to the lungs, just as frustration and rage block the flow of blood to the heart. Many diseases, including asthma, ulcers, and high blood pressure, are triggered by stress and can be alleviated by such stress-reduction techniques as biofeedback and meditation.

The immune system is our body's natural defense to repel an invasion against germs, pollutants, and foreign substances. We are constantly under attack by microscopic organisms seeking to invade our bloodstream and vital organs. These organisms that don't belong in our body are called "antigens" and include viruses, bacteria, and parasites. A healthy immune system keeps us from succumbing to infections and diseases caused by these organisms. Our first line of defense is our skin and mucous membranes. If antigens get past the skin and mucous membranes, they face the second defense system, the scavenger and killer cells, which attack any organism recognized as foreign to the body. The third form of protection consists of T-cells, which recognize and interact with specific targets, and B-cells, which produce antibodies designed to attack specific antigens. These antibodies produced by the B-cells may remain in the body to provide immunity against future onslaughts by the same antigen.

The immune system sometimes malfunctions and reacts to relatively harmless antigens like dust or pollen, causing an allergic reaction. Sometimes it may mistakenly attack the body's own cells and organs; this results in such diseases as diabetes, rheumatoid arthritis, and systemic lupus. The immune system may also break down if it becomes overwhelmed by the number and strength of the invading organisms or if it is missing one or more of its key fighters. This disorder may be temporary and can be caused by such trauma as surgery or stress. The HIV virus causes a chronic disorder of the immune system which destroys or disables the body's T-cells, making the patient vulnerable to deadly infections and cancers.

There are ways in which we can contribute to the health of our immune system. We can eat a variety of wholesome foods, especially fruits, vegetables, whole grains, and low-fat dairy products. We can exercise to strengthen the body's resistance to infection and disease. We can make sure that we get plenty of sleep, because it is one of the body's best defenses against infection. We can strive to be optimistic and stress free. Just as our thoughts and emotions can induce illness, they can also determine the effectiveness of our immune system and the body's resistance to infection. When we learn to control our mind and emotions, we can begin to control our immune system.

When my Higher Self first told me that we not only create all of our illnesses, but we are also responsible for our own healing, I rejected the idea. The more I studied, the more I realized that this is really true. If we create our own reality, then we are responsible for our health and well-being. All healing is achieved by means of natural laws that are innate within our bodies. A physician may sew up a severe cut or set a broken bone, but the doctor does not perform the healing. The healing comes from within the body of the individual. By listening to our inner self, we will be able to mobilize all the healing powers that lie within us.

Many of us feel a need to have a logical, reasonable explanation for an illness or accident. We believe that if we understand why this happened to us, we can handle the experience better. Sometimes we need to ask ourselves if we are gaining attention or avoiding something by being ill. Maybe our illness gives us a certain amount of power over other people. When we can't discover an acceptable reason, we may have a feeling that our suffering is really unfair. Others may see their illness or accident as a sign of a personal failure or a form of punishment. Now is the time to let go of any feelings of helplessness or guilt. It's up to us to decide how we will interpret our suffering. Is it a punishment, or an opportunity to learn a lesson we chose for our own spiritual growth?

Past events have helped to create our current thoughts, attitudes, and actions. The medical profession accepts the fact that many adult illnesses have their origins in childhood. How parents respond to their children's illnesses, and how they deal with their own ailments, have a long-term influence on their children's behavior. Because we are also influenced by our past lives, some illnesses may have their origin in another life at another time. Our health could be affected by a lesson that still needs to be learned or a karmic debt that must be resolved.

Regardless of the causes of our physical problems, all of us have healing energies within our bodies. After taking a placebo, people often experience pain relief and rapid healing. These positive effects are not caused by the sugar pill but by the person's own expectations. A placebo not only looks like a powerful medication, it acts like one, too. Our *belief* that this pill will bring healing generates chemical changes within the body which trigger the release of pain-fighting chemicals called endorphins.

There is a powerful healing energy available to all of us that comes from our Higher Self. It's difficult to describe something that is pure spirit. Psychically it appears to be streams of white light with sparkles of silver swirling through it. The source of the White Light is the God Essence of our Higher Self. Some call it the inflowing of the Holy Spirit. This White Light is an electromagnetic force that can be absorbed by the body, bringing us healing and protection.

This method of healing is simple yet extremely effective. *First*, while in the meditative state, ask your Higher Self for God's healing energy. *Second*, picture the energy entering your crown center and flowing through all of your bodies, bringing peace and healing to every cell. This healing process can take from five to thirty minutes. You may even feel a tingling in your hands and feet as the energy flows through you. *Third*, when the energy stops flowing, thank your Higher Self for the healing.

Sometimes our emotional response to sickness or injury is fear, worry, or anger. No matter how strong we may be, there is some element of *victim* within each of us. Just when strength and courage are needed the most, we may be the most vulnerable. It's important that we have someone to lean on in our time of emotional and physical weakness, especially if we are hospitalized. Since we may be too sick to assert ourselves when we are in the hospital, it is important that we choose a family member or a friend to act as our advocate. We not only need someone to comfort and encourage us; we also need someone by our side to ensure that we receive the proper medication and to discuss treatment options with our doctor. After an operation several years ago, my doctor signed a release for me to leave the hospital. I was too ill to object, but my daughter stood up for me and let him know that I was still too weak to be sent home.

Every once in awhile, I meet someone who thinks it is a kind of moral or ethical weakness to see a doctor or to take any medication. They tell me that they are not comfortable with modern medicine. We need to consider every possible method to encourage our body to heal itself, whether it is seeing a medical or holistic doctor, taking herbal or traditional medication, using acupressure or acupuncture, hypnosis, meditation, massage, or chiropractic adjustment. By listening to the inner self, we will be able to mobilize all the healing powers that lie within us.

Over the past two decades, alternative medicine has gained recognition as a healing method. Many feel that we are headed for a new era of intergraded medicine, in which the best of Western medicine will be combined with alternative methods of healing. We should not disregard Western medicine, because it is an important partner in the healing process. When we experience any urgent problem, such as a possible fracture, serious infection, or worrisome change in our health, we need to consult our primary physician. Alternative therapies are helpful in the healing process because most of them tap into the body's natural defense system and pose little risk to the patient. Some of the best-known alternative therapies are acupuncture, chiropractic medicine, biofeedback therapy, hypnosis, massage therapy, reflexology, acupressure, and homeopathic and herbal remedies.

Some authors and teachers have long lists of illnesses that they associate with a particular action or emotion. For example, they say that the common cold results from self-pity, heart attacks are caused by hate, cancer is activated by prolonged anxiety, and ulcers are caused not by what you eat but by "what is eating you." To a degree, this is correct, but I feel that there is no universal cause that can be identified in all cases of a certain illness. Even though we are responsible for our illness, there's no reason to feel guilty for being sick or for not getting well. The natural response to illness is often anxiety and depression. That's scary enough without carrying the extra load of guilt. We need to face these negative thoughts and put them into the proper perspective.

We needn't waste time trying to figure out why we became ill. Rather than asking what we did to cause our illness, it's more important to ask what we can learn from this experience. Illness can be an opportunity to become more self-aware. It can be part of our transformation process. Sometimes a cure is not possible. There's a difference between being cured and being healed. Healing occurs at an emotional and spiritual level and involves fitting the disease into our life pattern.

If faced with a chronic health condition or a terminal illness, we can join a support group where we will be able to talk openly about what's worrying us without feeling that we're burdening or scaring anyone. Holding back our emotions will just put an added strain on the body. Sharing openly can help to defuse our fear and anxiety. It's important that we acknowledge what we're going through. We also need to live fully in the here-and-now, hoping for and expecting the best.

Now more than ever before, it is imperative that we are in charge of all decisions concerning our health. If we are faced with surgery or a questionable procedure, we should get a second and perhaps a third opinion. We need to choose a doctor who will not only listen to us but will also explain in detail the options that are available.

As we approach enlightenment, more healing information will flow into our minds from the Higher Beings. We will learn healing techniques that were once known only in the higher realms. We are beginning to understand more about the healing power of light and sound. With the use of light and sound, the physical, energy, emotional, and soul body can be healed and brought into a complete state of balance.

As our bodies are adjusting to the physical transformations that will be occurring, we need to be as healthy as possible. To maintain a healthy body, it is necessary for us to make spiritual love the primary expression of our life. We need to love, nurture, and encourage ourselves. It's important that we see our life as our own creation and hold positive images and goals in our mind. We need to accept ourselves and everything in our life as an opportunity for growth and learning. Then we need to foster loving friendships and relationships. We can do things for others that will bring us a sense of fulfillment and that make a positive contribution to our family, friends, and community.

It is important that we release all negative emotions — hatred, guilt, resentment, envy, fear, sadness, anger. We need to heal any wounds incurred in past relationships. If we seem to fail in some undertaking, we can still learn from the experience, and then forgive ourselves and move on.

It is also important that we nourish our bodies with healthful food and maintain a healthy weight. In addition, taking a sensible amount of vitamin supplements can be beneficial. Our body also needs at least eight glasses of water a day to remain healthy. It's time to let go of any negative habits such as smoking, drinking alcoholic beverages, or taking harmful drugs, because they affect all of our bodies and impede our spiritual progress. It's important that we exercise not only our body but also our mind. Finally, we need to believe in the possibility of total health and then make a commitment toward achieving that goal so that we will be ready for the transformations that will occur within our bodies as we prepare for the higher vibrations of the fourth dimension.

2

Recharging the Energy Body

Physical
Energy (Etheric)

One of my favorite television commercials is the Energizer bunny who "just keeps going and going." However, our own energy body needs to be recharged nightly. This is especially important at this time because of the stress on our physical body as cells and molecules are being restructured and the frequency is being increased. As our body goes through these changes, we may find that we need more sleep than usual. Therefore, it's important not only that we have a good night's sleep, but also that we take time during the day for rest and relaxation.

Some people refer to the energy body as the "etheric double." I use the terms "energy" and "etheric" body interchangeably. The energy body is about an inch larger than the physical body and interpenetrates it. The two bodies are connected at the navel area by a very short cord. The energy body cannot act as a separate body and is unable to leave the physical body and travel independently.

A physical body is not complete without its etheric counterpart, which is a replica of the physical form. Neither can exist without the other. We can compare the physical and energy body to a flashlight. The outside, lens, globe, and switch are like the physical body. But the light does not go on until we put in the batteries — the energy body. If the batteries are weak, the light becomes dim and finally goes out.

The energy body is composed of electromagnetic energy, the life force also known as "prana." The purpose of the energy body is to absorb the life force or prana and distribute it to the physical body. This life force is best described as vitality and is the integrating energy that coordinates the physical cells and holds them together. If it were not for the presence of prana, there could be no physical body as an integral whole. This life energy emanates from the Sun. When sunlight is abundant, prana also appears in abundance. When there is less sunlight, as in the winter, the supply of prana is at a lower level.

A person who for some reason lacks a sufficient amount of prana frequently and unconsciously absorbs vitality from someone who is nearby. This is the reason we sometimes feel drained of energy when we are near a person who has a low level of vitality, especially someone who is ill or elderly. We are usually willing to give of our energy to those we love when they need a boost of vitality. However, because we do not want others draining our vitality, we need to protect the energy body. This lesson was brought home to me very clearly when I volunteered in a nursing home and experienced a tremendous difference in my level of energy. Usually I remembered to surround myself with the White Light of protection from my Higher Self. At the end of the day, I would feel pleased that I had brought joy into the lives of some of the patients. However, on the days when I forgot to visualize myself surrounded with the White Light, I would feel drained — not only physically, but emotionally as well.

Although the energy body is colorless and invisible, it is possible to feel it. With a partner, close your eyes, become quiet, and without touching the other person, feel the space around him. As you experiment, you will discover that there is a different feeling between the emotional body and energy body.

During the early 1930s my dad saw many etheric bodies, although at the time he did not realize what they were. During the depression, jobs were so hard to find that my father had to take a position in the morgue at the Los Angeles General Hospital. This giant monolith served as the last stop for many poor, homeless people. Dad's job was to collect the dead bodies from the wards and take them down to the morgue in the basement. From an early age, I was impressed with the stories that my father told of seeing a ghostly cloud or haze hovering over many of the dead bodies. This cloud was the energy body, which continues to have life within it for a period of time after the physical body has died. For this reason, many religions believe that there should be a three-day waiting period before cremation or burial to give the energy body time to wind down and die.

Sleep restores energy to the body. When we fall asleep, our muscles relax and our heartbeat and breathing slow down. During the night we experience three or four cycles of sleep, varying from light through medium to a very deep state. During certain periods of sleep, our eyes move rapidly as we watch the events of a dream that our Higher Self is presenting to us. This dream state is called "REM" sleep, which is short for "Rapid Eye Movement." It is during an even deeper period of sleep that our astral body is able to leave the physical body and go exploring on its own. As our energy body is being recharged, our consciousness is often active in the astral body.

Our sleep requirements are probably something we're born with, and they vary from individual to individual. Although the average person needs about eight hours sleep a night, the time may vary from a minimum of four to a maximum of ten hours. If you wake up groggy, you may be a person who is not getting enough sleep. The criterion of a good night's sleep may have less to do with how long we have slept than how rested and refreshed we feel the next morning.

All of us have probably had a sleepless night from time to time. If you occasionally have a restless, sleepless night, don't worry. The energy body will catch up on the sleep it needs in a few days. Inability to go to sleep can result from a number of causes. Indigestion or overexcitement may lead to insomnia. Pain or discomfort from a physical illness will also interfere with sleep. Coffee or other stimulants can cause insomnia. Certain drugs affect the brain in such a way as to produce wakefulness. Drinking wine, beer, or other alcoholic beverages tends to relax people and put them to sleep, but several hours later as the alcohol withdraws from the brain, they may become wide awake.

If you have insomnia and can't pinpoint the cause, try keeping a sleep diary, including what you eat and drink before bedtime, when you go to bed, how long before you fall asleep, and how often you wake up during the night. You may be able to discover a pattern to your sleep problems.

Some insomniacs are sleepless because of psychological problems. They say that if they could just stop their thoughts they could fall asleep. Instead, they lie awake obsessing about work, family, a lost job, or money problems. Their body tunes in to their growing despair, and their muscles tighten, while heart rate and body temperature climb. Then they begin worrying about whether they'll ever get to sleep.

A client of mine came to me with a problem of insomnia. I asked her how she prepared for sleep, and she told me that each night when she went to bed she had a life-long habit of saying her prayers. By the time she had prayed for her six adult children and her eight grandchildren, she was wide awake and filled with worries and fears about their future. I suggested that she say her prayers in the morning instead of at night. Several weeks later she called me and said that this simple change in her life had cured her insomnia.

As we grow older, we may find it harder to get to sleep. Women who are pregnant or experiencing menopause may have trouble falling asleep or staying asleep because of the hormonal changes that are occurring within the body. Chronic sleep deprivation can result in irritability, slowed thinking, problems with memory, decreased response time, difficulty paying attention, and lack of energy. Whatever the cause of your sleep disturbance, it is important that you discuss long-term insomnia with your doctor and get the problem resolved as soon as possible.

Something that I have found helpful in getting a good night's sleep is keeping a notepad by my bed. Often I get a message from my Higher Self while I'm sleeping. It can be an answer to a question I've asked, or a good idea, or a new way of looking at a certain problem. I keep going over and over the information in my mind until I write it down. Then it's as if my Higher Self is assured that I did receive the message, and I can get back to sleep.

Some people depend on over-the-counter sleeping pills for a good night's sleep. These can help you through a rough night or two, but they may leave you feeling groggy the next day. Over a period of several days, your body may become tolerant of them. Others use prescription drugs to combat their insomnia, but these can be habit-forming. Most sleep aids that are taken regularly lose their effectiveness. Some people, however, have found that herbal sleep aids are effective without being habit-forming.

When you try very hard to do something over which you have no control, such as falling asleep, you may become anxious. This only makes things worse. If you are in bed for half an hour and can't get to sleep, it is better to get up before panic sets in. Anything is better than lying wide awake worrying if you'll ever get to sleep. So take your mind off the problem by reading or watching television. This will give your body a chance to become sleepy naturally.

It is important that we have the proper environment for sleep. As we evolve spiritually and the vibrations of our body are raised, we may become even more sensitive to sound. So a barking dog, loud music, or the snoring of a mate can keep us awake. If the noise is beyond our control, we may need to resort to earplugs, or a machine that produces the sound of ocean waves or rain on the roof. This "white noise" may help to muffle the irritating noise.

Most people sleep better in a darkened room that is well ventilated and kept at a comfortable temperature. A comfortable bed and pillows also help us to sleep better. My Higher Self has warned me against using an electric blanket during the night, so I have compromised by turning it on only in winter to warm my bed before I go to sleep.

To get a good night's sleep, it's important that we practice good sleep habits. If you feel the need for a nap during the day, keep it short. Sleeping longer than thirty minutes can leave a person groggy and interfere with getting to sleep at night. Avoid alcohol and anything that is caffeinated for several hours before bedtime. Not only coffee, but also tea, some soft drinks, dark chocolate, diuretics, and some cold and allergy medications contain large amounts of caffeine. The nicotine in cigarettes is a stimulant and also interferes with sleep. Exercise is important, but not late in the day. If you are unusually fatigued, you may be too worn out or keyed up to go to sleep.

We each need to develop a personal nightly routine. Take time to relax before going to bed. Focus your thoughts on a peaceful scene. Do some deep breathing. Meditate. Take a warm, leisurely bath. Enjoy a glass of milk. Alert your body that it's time to go to sleep. This may be as simple as showering, brushing your teeth, reading a chapter in a book or doing a crossword puzzle. Most important, try to go to bed at the same time each night.

Our energy can be depleted in a variety of ways. One of the most common causes of exhaustion is trying to do too much. So learn to pace yourself and when your body says rest … listen! Make sure that your fatigue isn't caused by medication. Ask your doctor about possible side effects of any medications that you are taking. Some antidepressants and antihistamines can cause fatigue. A common cause of fatigue is not eating good nutritious meals, or skipping meals altogether. Surprisingly, low fluid intake is a common but often overlooked cause of fatigue. It is important that we drink at lease eight glasses of water a day.

When stress or boredom leads to fatigue, social contact can be uplifting. Call or visit a friend. Do something nice for yourself. When we are involved in doing something that we really enjoy, we seem to experience a surge of energy. It is also true that vitality springs from commitment and service to others.

Exercise does not deplete our energy unless we overexert ourselves. In fact, if the cause of our exhaustion is anxiety, grief, or boredom, exercise can generally help restore our energy. When we are fatigued, the mere thought of a workout may be exhausting, but exercise is actually one of the most effective ways to boost our energy level. Aerobic exercise strengthens the heart and lungs, which in turn improves oxygen circulation throughout the body and boosts energy production at the cellular level.

Spending time meditating in a quiet room with our eyes closed can induce profound relaxation, which in turn will result in our feeling less tired and more alert. This is an excellent method of recharging the energy body.

Chronic fatigue can be a symptom of a serious medical or psychological condition that only a doctor can diagnose. Fatigue is a classic symptom of clinical depression. An underactive thyroid gland can cause fatigue and slow metabolism. The earliest symptoms of anemia or iron deficiency are fatigue and irritability. Chronic fatigue immune dysfunction syndrome (CFIDS) is still largely a mystery illness. People with CFIDS are not only debilitated by fatigue but may experience other symptoms such as headaches, blurred vision, fevers, and short-term memory loss.

Biorhythm is the behavioral science of life-energy rhythms. The energy body is affected by these biorhythms.

This results in a fluctuation of energy during different times of the day. It also determines whether someone is a morning or night person. It is important that we understand our personal energy swings and plan our day accordingly. When we keep irregular hours, we throw our internal rhythms askew. The body becomes confused and may be primed for action just when it's time to go to sleep. That is why jet lag can make us feel so tired; it is also the reason why we need to keep as regular a sleep schedule as possible.

Most of us have experienced days when we wake up in the morning feeling terrific and other days when we are almost too tired to get out of bed. This is due partly to the fact that we not only have daily internal rhythms but other cycles as well: the physical-energy cycle is about twenty-eight days long; an emotional cycle is about thirty-two days long; a mental or intellectual cycle is thirty-six days long; and the little-known spiritual cycle is forty days long. Each cycle begins the day we are born and continues throughout the rest of our life. Even the ancient physician Hippocrates advised his followers to observe the regular fluctuations of good and bad days and to take this into account when treating a patient. When we understand our inner biological clock, we are better able to pace our mental, physical, and emotional activities.

Calculators and computer programs simplify the mathematics of biorhythms. About ten years ago my daughter gave me a biorhythm calculator which I used until the batteries went dead a couple of years later. Then I began to understand my cycles by listening to my body. I found this to be as helpful as using my calculator. On the days that I have a lot of energy, I accomplish a great deal more than during my low-energy periods. When I'm tired, I don't feel guilty about taking it easy.

During part of the twenty-eight days of the physical-energy cycle, we are filled with energy and have greater strength and endurance, as well as better resistance to infection and disease. Then as the cycle draws to a close, we may become more tired than usual. Low-energy days leave us vulnerable to disease and infection, so it is important that we conserve our energy and take life easy. Just knowing that high days are surely coming can help us get through the low times. By understanding our biorhythms, we will be in better harmony with the energy body.

Just as the physical body possesses seven centers called the endocrine glands, the energy or etheric body also has seven energy centers. These vortexes of energy are sometimes referred to as "chakras," meaning "wheels of energy." The etheric centers and the physical glands interpenetrate each other. The physical glands are affected by the energy or prana drawn into the etheric centers. In turn, the etheric centers are influenced by the hormones produced by the glands. Each can absorb the substances that will harmonize with the vibrational qualities of the Soul inhabiting the physical body. As we progress spiritually, our etheric centers will become increasingly more active.

The endocrine glands manufacture and secrete hormones directly into the bloodstream. These hormones affect growth, the shape of the body, the way the body uses food, and the way the body adjusts to changes in the environment. Each endocrine gland produces one or more hormones which, in a healthy body, are released at the proper time, in the proper amount, into the bloodstream. The energy centers produce etheral hormones which are sent through the etheric bloodstream to the other centers in the energy body and to the glands in the physical body. Working together, the etheric centers and the physical glands regulate the development and health of the body.

Although some teachers may identify different glands with the energy centers and use different names and colors for those centers, the concept is the same. The energy vortexes of those who have not yet begun their spiritual journey move sluggishly and the colors are dull. In those who are already walking the spiritual path, the energy is pulsating and the colors are brilliant and pure.

The first of these energy centers is called the sexual or root center. It superimposes the reproductive glands of the physical body. From this etheric center, the red ray flows to the reproductive organs. If people keep their thoughts and emotions focused on selfish, lustful sexual activities, the etheric center develops a murky, muddy red color. Those who transmute sexual emotions into pure love will cause the red ray of this center to become a soft rose color.

The second energy center is called the navel center. It superimposes the pancreas, which is situated almost directly behind the stomach. This center is the connecting point between the energy body and the physical body. Through this center much of the energy (prana) is drawn into the body. It is an extremely active center and vibrates in various shades of orange. This etheric center sends energy to the liver, kidneys, and intestines. When the navel center is fully activated, we become more sensitive and consciously aware of astral influences.

The third energy center, the solar plexus center, superimposes the adrenal glands of the physical body. This is the connecting point between the emotional (astral) and physical bodies and is probably the most sensitive of all the centers. The shades of yellow within this center vary with each individual's spiritual growth. When this etheric center is fully activated, we can remember some of our nightly astral journeys, perhaps as very vivid dreams. We may even begin to consciously leave the physical body and travel astrally.

The fourth energy center is the heart center, which superimposes the thymus gland. This etheric center is the midway point between the three lower and the three higher centers. It is the bridge between the physical and the spiritual centers. The color of this center radiates various shades of green which are influenced by the type of love the person expresses. The heart is the center of compassion and empathy, as well as love. When this center is activated, it makes a person consciously aware of the joys and sorrows of others. As we learn to love unconditionally, this center will begin to vibrate on a higher frequency.

The fifth etheric center is the throat center, which superimposes the thyroid gland. The blue ray of this center gives health to the region of the throat and vocal chords. This is the center of inspiration and higher ideals. Someone whose throat center is fully activated may become clairaudient. This is the ability of intuitively hearing those in a higher dimension. With the gift of clairaudience comes the ability to channel the messages that are intuitively heard.

The sixth energy center is the brow center, is located at a point almost directly between the eyebrows and linked to the pineal gland. This center emits a violet ray. It has been called the seat of intuition because, when this center becomes active, we begin to be in tune with our Higher Self and other Masters. When the brow center is awakened, a person may become clairvoyant and have the ability to tune in to the higher dimensions.

The seventh etheric center is the crown center, which lies at the top of the head and extends upward, radiating pure white light. This center is the gateway through which the highest spiritual essences enter the body. It is the connecting point through which our Higher Self not only communicates with us but also sends us healing and protecting energies. When this center is fully open, it signals the awakening of our mastership and enlightenment.

It is possible to help stimulate these energy vortexes during meditation by directing attention to individual centers and visualizing the purest form of the color connected with that center. As we continue our spiritual pilgrimage to enlightenment and live a balanced physical, mental, emotional, and spiritual life, all our centers will become *fine-tuned* to a higher frequency.

When all the energy centers are activated and vibrating on this higher frequency, the electromagnetic current will begin to flow upward. Beginning at the sexual center, this life force travels through each center in turn as it gathers energy, until it reaches the crown center, where it streams forth in all its glory. This has been referred to as "raising the *kundalini*." Esoteric teachers of past generations have warned against the student trying to force the *kundalini* energy to flow until all their centers are completely open. When a person is finally ready, this flow of energy will occur spontaneously during meditation. The nearest way to describe this feeling of spiritual ecstasy is to liken it to a loving sexual climax. Like a sexual climax, we would not desire to be in such a state all the time. It is during this special time, as the electromagnetic current flows upward through our centers, that we can begin to comprehend our true self.

When we realize that without the energy body the physical body would not be able to survive, we can understand why the health of the energy body is so important. We can also understand why both our energy and physical bodies need to work together as a unit. To have a healthy energy body, it is important that we are in tune with our internal biorhythms and that we faithfully recharge the energy body by getting the proper amount of sleep. As our etheric centers are activated and vibrating on a higher frequency, we will be closer to our goal of achieving enlightenment.

3

Balancing the Emotional Body

Physical
Energy (Etheric)
Emotional (Astral)

When I was growing up there was a popular song whose lyrics were, "You've got to accentuate the positive, eliminate the negative." What wonderful advice this is, because there really are only two types of emotions — positive and negative. Positive emotions include love, joy, delight, and hope. These emotions uplift the spirit. Negative emotions — anger, fear, despair, sadness, and worry — can make a person unhappy or depressed.

The Greeks were the first to discover that a human possesses a body which is a replica of the physical body but is made of a more ethereal substance. Aristotle thought that this body resembled the substance of stars, so it was named "astral," which means "starry." However, a more accurate name would be the "emotional body," because it responds to our every emotion. I use the names "astral" and "emotional" body interchangeably. The astral body interpenetrates the physical and energy bodies and extends several inches farther. A cord connects the emotional to the physical body at the solar plexus area. This cord is composed of an ethereal substance that is capable of stretching around the world. This makes it possible for us to leave the physical body behind and go exploring in the astral body.

Most physical illnesses really begin in the emotional body. That is the reason it is so important for us to learn how to balance the emotional body. When we get a bruise, it turns black and blue and gradually fades away. Unlike the physical body, when the emotional body is bruised, it does not heal with time. That is why some people are still carrying around bruises in the emotional body that occurred in childhood. These emotional hurts directly affect the physical body, causing different kinds of reactions and illnesses. Even if the physical body has been cured of an illness, if the emotional body has not been healed it will again cause some type of physical problem.

It's almost impossible not to feel depressed, angry or anxious at times in life, but we don't need to dwell on these negative emotions. Because normal emotions are usually fleeting, they are unlikely to cause health problems. The villains are the negative emotions of longer duration that trigger physical and chemical changes in the body. If these changes continue for a long period of time, damage to the body can result.

Some strong emotions cause parts of the nervous system to send signals to various glands and organs. Different hormones that are released cause varying changes in the body. When people become very angry or frightened, the hormones flow from the adrenal glands into the bloodstream. The hormones adrenaline and norepinephrine produce changes that would help anyone who was preparing for a fight or flight. The person's heart beats faster and more strongly, the blood pressure rises, and the bronchial tubes dilate to allow breathing to be quicker and easier. The liver releases more sugar into the bloodstream and the body burns oxygen more rapidly, which also provides an extra spurt of energy. Anger raises blood cholesterol and causes other changes that can lead to blockages in the arteries that nourish the heart.

Anger isn't the only dangerous emotion. Chronic pessimism, hopelessness, loneliness, anxiety, and depression put the body into a state that makes it harder to resist illnesses and could lead to potentially fatal diseases such as cancer and heart attacks. Those who habitually respond negatively to life are not only more likely to develop a variety of diseases, but they also recover more slowly. All emotions, both negative and positive, affect the emotional body.

The healing salve for wounds in the emotional body is love. This is available to us simply by asking our Higher Self to channel the healing energy of love through our crown center and then letting it flow through all our bodies, bringing peace and healing to every cell.

The part of the astral body that extends past the physical and energy bodies is often referred to as our aura. All living plants, animals, and humans have an astral body and an aura. The electromagnetic field that emanates from the emotional body can be photographed by using Kirlian photography. This is a process of photographing the aura by exposing it to a high-frequency electrical field. In the 1970s I took part in an experiment at the University of Southern California to test the differences in the discharge of light surrounding the touching fingertips of couples in love and of a pair of strangers. The black-and-white pictures of strangers showed very little energy flowing between them; however, there was a stream of electromagnetic energy reaching out and joining the fingertips of lovers. This demonstrated that the patterns of the auric field vary according to the person's emotions. In another experiment using Kirlian photography, pictures of leaves that had been cut in half clearly showed the aura of the whole leaf. Even though half of the physical part of the leaf was gone, the astral part was still intact.

The aura is composed of a fluctuating array of colors. These colors are affected by our thoughts, emotions, health, and spirituality. The aura is always moving and the colors are constantly melding into one another. The various colors sometimes disappear, only to return at another time. The more spiritual a person is, the clearer and richer the colors appear. People who are not on the spiritual path of love have duller colors. Illness and depression produce gray overtones in the aura. In the case of a sudden shock, the colors fade out and the whole emotional body takes on a grayish hue. The aura reacts immediately to our emotions. A sudden rush of emotions may flood the aura with a different color that pertains to the particular emotion being experienced. For example, intense anger produces black with streaks of red; jealousy has a greenish-brown hue; fear is gray; devotion is blue; pride is orange; and, of course, true love is a beautiful rose-pink.

When decorating the home or office, we need to keep in mind how colors in our environment affect our emotions. When I was teaching, I used yellow on the bulletin board in the classroom to enhance the children's intellect. However, too much yellow can become exhausting to the mind. Blue is a calming color, but too much blue can cause depression. In my living room I have an emerald green rug. Green can be used at any time and in any amount because it is a balanced color. A clear red is good if you need strength and stamina. However, red is not recommended for anyone who is tense or nervous. White, of course, is always effective as a neutral color.

The clothes we wear affect not only our aura but also our emotions. If you feel stressed, consider wearing greens and blues, which have a calming effect. If you need an energy boost, try wearing clothes with the colors red, orange, and yellow. Because of the negative effect the colors black and gray have on the aura, they need to be offset with bright colors, especially near the face.

To observe the true colors of the aura, we need to remove our clothes or wear something white. The wall behind us should be white and the lighting dim — either a candle or a lamp with a small yellow bulb. Enter the alpha state, and with eyes half closed, stare steadily into a large mirror. Seeing an aura is as much a sensing as it is a visual experience.

The physical colors of the aura have astral counterparts which are the opposite of the colors that appear to our physical eyes. This astral counterpart is seen with our inner sense of sight. The counterpart of orange is blue; red is green; yellow is purple; and white is gold. This may explain why there is sometimes a difference in the colors observed in the aura and in the etheric centers by various spiritual teachers: some are seeing the colors from the third dimension, and some from the fourth.

This fact was brought to my attention one summer day as I was driving along a Los Angeles freeway. All of a sudden, I was seeing astral houses and trees in the middle of the freeway. My instinct was to take the nearest off-ramp until I could adjust my sight back to the physical dimension. At the bottom of the off-ramp was a signal and the light was green, so I continued on through the intersection. Behind me I heard the siren of a police car signaling me to pull over. When the policeman approached my car, he asked if I had noticed the red light I had just gone through. Obviously, I couldn't explain to him that the counterpart of the red light appeared to me to be green. So I accepted the ticket and went on my way. Luckily, this is the only time I have had an experience like this.

Anger is a basic human emotion which not only causes a reaction in the aura and the emotional body, but also causes changes in the physical body. In early times, the emotion of anger was often necessary for survival. In modern times, it is important for us to understand how to manage our anger. When someone says or does something to hurt us, we may feel merely irritated and annoyed by their actions, or we may be so angry that we have thoughts and feelings of hostility and revenge. Chronic anger is unhealthy. If we don't express our anger productively, we may harbor inner resentment and fury. If we repress our anger, eventually it will take its toll on our physical and emotional health. Those who suppress their anger are more likely to die of cardiovascular disease or cancer than someone who freely expresses feelings in a productive manner.

When someone hurts us, instead of immediately responding with anger or hatred, we can take a deep breath and ask ourselves if the situation is really serious enough to get worked up over. Will getting angry make a difference? How can we use our anger in a productive way? Besides counting to ten before saying or doing something, we can take a walk or close our eyes and concentrate on our breathing. In this way, we will have had time to see the situation more clearly.

We need to be honest about the anger or hatred that we feel. We may decide to approach the person responsible for our anger and tell them why we feel so upset. Another way is to pour out our anger and bitterness by writing a letter to the person who has enraged us. Then put the letter aside. Writing unsent letters is a harmless, healthy way to acknowledge our anger. After a time, when we have worked through our anger, we will probably tear up the letters and put the whole experience behind us. Letting go of the incident is really important, because there is nothing more fruitless than continually replaying a past, hurtful experience. If the problem is partly our fault, we need to admit it and then let go of the guilt as well as the anger.

When we are angry at someone, rather than taking it personally, we may decide to view the whole experience from a different, impersonal perspective and realize that for some reason we have invited this experience into our life as a lesson we have chosen to learn.

Forgiveness is a way to set ourselves free from the negative emotions of anger and hate. All of us at some time in our lives have struggled with a need to forgive someone. Even though we feel that we should forgive, many of us don't know how to forgive. Let's say that our mate has been unfaithful, how do we forgive? Do we play the role of victim and say, "I'll forgive you even though I know you'll keep on hurting me"? Out of fear, do we say, "I'll forgive you because I don't want to lose my marriage"? Perhaps the forgiveness is conditional: "I'll forgive you, but I'm still holding onto my resentments." Perhaps we are patronizing: "I forgive you because you don't know any better." We do have free will. We can choose to hold onto our hurts and resentments, or we can let them go with love. True forgiveness is unconditional.

One of my clients has been divorced for more than ten years and is still angry with her ex-husband. She told me, "I'll never forgive him for what he did to me." I have tried to explain to her that, until we forgive those who have hurt us, they will continue to cause us pain. We do not need to approve of them to forgive them. We do not even need to like them. We just need to understand that they are human and, therefore, make mistakes. We need to let go of the desire to prove we are right and to release our anger and bitterness.

Forgiveness does not mean that we accept cruel behavior or that we will continue to let others hurt us. It does not mean that we will pretend an incident did not happen or that we believe a person's actions are acceptable. Forgiveness means that we acknowledge human imperfection and can create harmony and love in spite of it.

If you are sincere in your goal of achieving enlightenment, it is important that you resolve all negative relationships. A negative relationship is one in which you feel anger, hatred, sorrow, guilt, or revenge toward someone. It could be a casual acquaintance in the course of which an unkind word was spoken, or you feel you were mistreated in some other way. Or it could be an extremely abusive relationship that continued over a long period of time. If you are unable to forgive and let go of the hurt, you will meet this other person again in another life to take care of the unfinished karma. All relationships must eventually end with unconditional love.

Forgiveness comes more easily when we understand that people are simply following their own path. We also need to remember that we brought these people into our life to help us learn an important lesson. We may not understand what that lesson is at this time. Perhaps we may never know as long as we remain in a physical body. But when we realize that everything is happening for a reason, we will experience a sense of peace and serenity. We can begin the process of committing ourselves to forgiving every person who has ever done us harm. It doesn't matter if the person we need to forgive is living or has already left the Earth through death. We can still forgive him.

Don't be discouraged if forgiveness seems difficult. It's hard for everyone at first. Sometimes it is so difficult that we need the help of our Higher Self to forgive. One method I have found helpful is to write down all the ways and times you have been hurt by the person you now wish to forgive. When you have completed the list, have a ceremony of forgiveness. Take the list outside and ask your Higher Self to help you forgive. Then set fire to the list. As it burns, let go emotionally of all the hurts and, with the help of your Higher Self, forgive that person. Because you are human, you may sometimes remember the emotional pain, but immediately remind yourself that through your Higher Self all has been forgiven.

When we forgive other people, they no longer have power to control us. Once we forgive, we no longer need to blame. Blame is the belief that others are responsible for our unhappiness; revenge is the action we take, or wish to take, to inflict suffering on the person we blame for hurting us. Though blame can be transcended and the desire for revenge banished, it's nearly impossible to completely stop judging people. When we accept people instead of judging them, we can put forgiveness into practice and eliminate our angry thoughts and feelings which could eventually create physical problems for us.

Grief, like anger, is an emotion that affects not only the emotional body but also the physical body. Normal grief can be experienced in several ways. At first there may be disbelief, especially when the cause of the grief is unexpected. Grief may show itself as a loss of appetite, repetition of thoughts, difficulty in sleeping, a tendency to sigh, and a continual feeling of tiredness. Sometimes there is anger. This anger may be directed toward someone else, or it may be directed inward because of a sense of guilt.

Crying is not only a natural reaction to grief — it is also therapeutic. When we explain our tears to children, they are then free to show their own grief. The expression of grief should not be repressed or delayed, for then it might find its outlet in a less desirable behavior. If we feel we must suppress our feelings or assume a brave front, we are adding one more burden to the many we already have at this time of emotional crisis. If we deny our emotions or keep them bottled up within us, we may later be faced with deep depression. Not all people express their grief in the same way. One may shed very few tears, while another will need to cry freely. Some may wish to be alone while others choose to be with friends and talk and cry together. It is important that we feel at ease with the method that best helps us to express and resolve our grief.

Someone who is grieving may become convinced that there is no way to overcome these deep feelings. There are, however, a few simple ways that can help us survive an emotional crisis. First, return to normal activities as soon as possible. Second, get some exercise. The fatigue of depression and grief is emotional not physical. If it is possible, go on a vacation with a friend. The change of scenery and activities may help. Next, do something to help someone else. This will take the emphasis off oneself. Finally, keep in mind that *time* can and does heal the wounds of grief.

When someone we love is separated from us, we are left with a great void in our life. We may feel engulfed with grief and loneliness. When a marriage is broken by divorce or death, the one who is left may feel lost or helpless, especially when there is a family to support. Later the survivor may become angry because she has been left alone with the burden of carrying on as head of the family.

Sometimes in the midst of our own agony, we may ignore the suffering of a child. A child's reaction to divorce or death is geared to his particular stage of development. He may react to his loss with feelings of anger, disbelief, panic, anxiety, or guilt. Perhaps the youngster is not able to express in words how he feels, so he may depend on overt behavior which an adult might feel is inappropriate. We should, however, take care not to shame or criticize our children for the responses they make when confronted with death or divorce.

A child may feel a sense of abandonment, or he may feel that in some way he is responsible for what has happened. If the child feels guilty or if he has some unresolved anxieties, he may exhibit such abnormal behavior as stammering, temper tantrums, or nightmares. It is extremely important for us to reassure the youngster that he is in no way responsible for the separation. We need to be aware of the child's pain and give him emotional support. The youngster should be given a chance to ask questions and to talk about his grief so that he can get all of his thoughts sorted out. If someone has died, the child needs to have an opportunity to discuss his memories of the person who has left and to talk about his feelings of personal loss. It is important that we reassure him that even though someone he loved is gone, that person remains very much alive in the hearts and memories of the family.

We, as adults, have the responsibility of supplying the emotional needs of our children during this time of grief by showing them empathy, understanding, and especially love. In this way we contribute to the child's feelings of security and give him the assurance that his world will eventually be back to normal. As soon as possible, all the members of the family need to return to their everyday routines of work or school. The necessity to carry on with our normal duties will assist the process of adjustment for both parents and child.

When faced with the death of someone we love, our hearts cry out in grief and loneliness. The mourning process can be made easier when we have a firm religious or spiritual belief that gives meaning to both life here and life in the World Beyond. It seems that it is not what the belief is, but how truly and genuinely it is believed, that enables people to accept death with a feeling of peace. In dealing with grief, the funeral service can serve a useful purpose in helping us to cope with the reality of death. This gives a safe framework within which we can express our grief. The funeral and other religious rites that we observe during the period of mourning can help to engage all our feelings of grief in such a way that it makes them not only acceptable, but also easily expressible. A funeral is not only a tribute to the one who has died but is also helpful for those who remain. It is a ceremony during which we may pay our respect to the deceased and comfort the survivors. It is important that relatives and friends have some way of showing their sympathy at this time. Such expression, if it is freely given and freely received, will be beneficial to all.

Sometimes, especially if the death has been sudden, the departed Soul is allowed to attend his own funeral in his astral body. My father was very much in evidence at his funeral and seemed pleased that so many of his friends and relatives had come to pay their respects. He also seemed appreciative of the praise he received for all the good he had accomplished in his life. Indeed, my dad was, and is, a very special person.

The period of mourning varies with each individual. However, as soon as possible, we need to emotionally release the one who has gone so that he may realize his full potential in the World Beyond. We should not bind him to the Earth plane by our grief, but release him in love and understanding.

In my counseling I meet many people who are facing extremely difficult times in their lives. The death of a child is probably the greatest tragedy any parent can experience. When Nancy came to me for help, she cried, "Oh, FranCelia, I'm so heartbroken, I don't know what to do. Why did my baby die? Why did this happen? Why? Why?"

In words punctuated with great sobs, Nancy told me, "I had to run to the store to buy some meat for dinner. When I looked in on little Jimmy, he was still taking his afternoon nap. So my husband, Bill, said to go ahead and he would listen for the baby. When I got back from the store, Bill told me there hadn't been a peep out of Jimmy. After I had started dinner, I went in to see if Jimmy was awake yet. I was really frightened when I noticed that the blanket was pulled up over his head. When I lifted up the cover, I saw Jimmy lying there so still and cold. I screamed for Bill to call 911, thinking that there might still be a chance my baby would start breathing again. But inside of me I knew it was too late. When the police came, they found that Bill was home alone with Jimmy when he died. They said that Bill would have to go down to the police station for questioning. Oh, FranCelia, I'm so heartbroken I don't know what to do." Together we wept over the loss of her precious six-month-old son.

"You know," Nancy said sadly, "I keep wondering if it is my fault Jimmy died. Maybe he was sick and I didn't know it. If I had taken him to the doctor for his check-up last week when I had the appointment, maybe he would still be alive."

"Nancy, instead of worrying and wondering, why don't you ask your doctor all these questions?" I replied. She took my suggestion and made an appointment for the coming Monday.

The doctor told her, "Nancy, your baby was one of thousands of infants who die each year in the United States of a mysterious malady which we commonly call 'Crib Death' or 'Sudden Infant Death Syndrome' (SIDS). It is one of the leading causes of death in babies. The syndrome affects infants between the ages of one week and two years, with a peak occurring around three months. We have thus far been unable to find any explanation or cause for these deaths. But let me assure you, Nancy, that you were in no way responsible for your baby's death. Many people still believe that the cause of crib deaths is suffocation, but investigations have found that even when infants are covered by bedding, the amount of oxygen is not reduced to the point of suffocation. So although Jimmy had a blanket over his face, this did not cause his death."

The doctor continued, "The problem of correctly identifying Sudden Infant Death Syndrome is complicated by the fact that some coroners believe this diagnosis is an easy way out when the supposed cause of death cannot be determined. No other cause of death leaves in its wake the self-doubt, guilt, and charges of criminal neglect that accompany crib deaths. I have known of marriages being broken up because a husband would not live with a wife who had 'let their baby die.' Other couples have refused to have more children because they feared their next baby might also die. Some parents spend years blaming themselves or others for their baby's death. Let me again reassure you, Nancy, that neither you nor your husband were in any way responsible for Jimmy's death."

"Thank you so much, doctor," said Nancy, "for taking your time to explain this to me."

"I'm glad to have been of help," the doctor replied. "It's hard enough to lose an infant without the parents having to go through life haunted by the possibility that some-how they might have averted the tragedy."

When Nancy arrived for her next appointment, her face was etched with grief as she said, "I miss my baby so much. I still can't understand why Jimmy died if there was nothing physically wrong with him."

"Sometimes, we can't understand why something like this happens," I told Nancy. "In fact, you may never know as long as you are in a physical body. But there is a reason! For the first year or so of life, a Soul is given the right to withdraw if the Higher Self realizes that something is wrong: not the right time ... not the right parents ... or the physical body is not suitable to contain the Soul. The cause of crib deaths seems to be directly connected with this natural law that permits the Soul to withdraw from a physical body during the first year or two of life. It is even possible that the Soul who withdrew, through death, can return to the same parents at a later time in a physical body that is better suited for the Soul's spiritual growth. This I know, Nancy, that right now Jimmy is safe in the Children's Heaven where he is being cared for with great love and tenderness."

One morning six months after Jimmy's death, Nancy called me to share her good news: she and Bill were expecting another baby at the end of the year. She told me, "We'll never forget our little Jimmy and we still miss him so much. Even though Jimmy was with us such a short while, he will always be special to us. Bill and I realize that it is time to let go of our grief. We are both excitedly preparing to welcome our new baby into our hearts and home."

Although disappointment is not as strong an emo-tion as grief or anger, it is often too painful to be ignored. It can be caused by not getting something we wanted and felt we deserved. Disappointment does hurt, but friends and family probably don't want to hear too much complaining about it. In fact, we may even feel slightly embarrassed at being upset over the incident. While it's true that sometimes bad things do happen, every one of those situations offers us an opportunity to learn how to overcome obstacles and attain our goals despite our disappointments.

There may be times when we feel that we are not in control of everything that happens to us; that some things are other people's fault; that we were in the wrong place at the wrong time; that family circumstances created our misery. It's time to let go of these excuses. We need to accept total responsibility for our lives, because the truth is that we are the sum total of all the choices we have made up until this moment.

When I was a teenager one summer at camp, I received a letter from my boyfriend telling me he had just gotten engaged to someone else. I felt devastated. Finally I told one of the camp counselors about my disappointment. With great insight, she said to me, "When God closes one door, He always opens another, and often this will lead to an even more fulfilling future." How right she was! I've never forgotten her wise words. As a counselor, I often tell my clients the same thing. When we are disappointed because things didn't go as we expected, our Higher Self may have something in store for us that is even better than we had planned.

Disappointment and regret go hand in hand. All of us have probably made choices that we later regretted: choosing the wrong mate; having an affair; worrying too much about work; or not managing finances wisely. However, it's a waste of time and emotional energy to dwell continually on past mistakes. The choices have been made, and there is really nothing to be accomplished by regretting our mistakes. Some people regret the choices they didn't make: staying in an unfulfilling job or marriage; not pursuing a hobby that they love; not spending more time with family and friends; not continuing their education; or not having children. Maybe it's not too late to make our dreams become a reality. Other people regret not choosing a healthier lifestyle, not getting enough sleep, eating the wrong kinds of food, smoking, or not getting enough exercise. There are those who hesitate to make the changes that would lead to a healthier way of living because they think it would take too much effort.

Some people regret having taken too many risks in their lives, while others regret that they haven't been more adventuresome. If you're too impulsive, it's wise to exercise more caution. If you're overly cautious, be spontaneous once in awhile. We can't change the past, but the future is ours to create anything we desire.

Regret can become a valuable teacher. It can help us learn from our mistakes and keep us from repeating them. Regret can serve as a wake-up call that something is wrong and that we need to make better choices. If making choices is difficult, we need to weigh the pros and cons of each of our options. When we have identified our options, with the help of our Higher Self, we can make the best choice possible.

Grief, regret, and disappointments can all lead to a feeling of depression. At one time or another, we have probably all experienced the negative emotion of depression. (I am not talking about clinical depression, which is a severe condition for which medication or hospitalization may be required.) Depression is a feeling of continuing sadness, despondency, or hopelessness. It may be caused by many of life's experiences, including a sense of failure, the loss of a job or loved one, illness, or disability. Usually time will bring recovery, but professional help may shorten the duration and enable the person to learn to cope with depression if it recurs.

If you feel depressed, put your needs first and pamper yourself. Focus on what's going to make you feel better and more empowered. By using laughter and courage to get you through a particular tough time, you will discover that, with the help of your Higher Self, you can survive anything and bounce back stronger than before. So keep fighting the depression with courage, with humor, and without shame.

One way to help overcome depression is to get up and do something: go for a walk, visit a friend, watch a good movie. Don't skip breakfast, because by noon you'll end up being fatigued and even more depressed. Listen to your favorite music. Even pleasant fragrances can lessen depression and anxiety. That's because the area of the brain responsible for smell interacts with the part that regulates emotions.

Taking a mini-vacation through meditation is another way to combat depression. Close your eyes, breathe deeply, and visualize a beautiful place. Imagine you are there. Notice what you are seeing, hearing, and feeling. Allow the good feeling to spread throughout your body. Then feel the arms of your Higher Self encircling you and radiating love and perfect peace.

Even though people on the spiritual path have long recognized that the pineal gland is the site of the third eye, until about thirty-five years ago it remained a mystery to doctors and scientists. Recently it has been discovered that the pineal gland can affect our emotions and moods. Researchers have discovered that the pineal gland is an active part of the endocrine system, producing the hormone melatonin, which they believe tells us when to sleep and when to wake up. At night the pineal secretes melatonin, peaking during the deepest sleep. With the first light of day, secretion slows dramatically.

Normally, the levels of melatonin also change with the seasons. However, for the millions of people who have been diagnosed with seasonal affective disorder, aptly called "SAD," the level of melatonin does not seem to change with the seasons, giving rise to winter depression. The onset of symptoms is clearly related to the lack of sunlight. The treatment is daily exposure to high-intensity artificial light plus medication. Some doctors are prescribing a small amount of melatonin to be taken at night. It has been found that when one uses melatonin, sleep is more natural and comes in a few minutes, leaving no morning hangover and helping to reduce depression.

Worry and fear are emotions that we create with our thoughts. Some people are more talented worriers than others because they have creative, vivid imaginations and can conjure up scary pictures in their heads. A cycle of worry occurs when we stay focused on the fear and never try to get to the solution. We need to be open and honest about our worries. Talking to a friend or counselor may provide a new perspective on our anxieties. We can learn to separate our imaginary anxieties from our real problems. We can also gain new insights which may help reduce our worries and, in turn, lessen our physical and emotional tensions.

Fear can make us imagine all sorts of terrible things, and most of the time they don't turn out nearly as badly as we had feared. Our mind is so powerful that when we send out strong thoughts of fear, we may draw to us the very experience that we are afraid will happen. Constant fear may result in stomach disorders, including ulcers. Phobias, insecurities, anxiety, stress, and frustrations are all connected to the emotion of fear. When we choose not to act because of fear, we begin to avoid life. We need to take some risks. or life becomes dull and boring.

If fear is the problem, faith is the solution. We can overcome fear by understanding that the indwelling power of our Higher Self is able to help us overcome any problem that we may encounter. Our goal, as we strive for enlightenment, is to be able to rise above our fears and live by faith.

In our fast-paced world, it seems that we meet some type of stress-filled situation around every corner. We may feel overworked, overwhelmed, and underappreciated. Our relationship with family and friends may add to our stress, which directly affects our physical body. Doctors aren't sure exactly how stress triggers stomach problems, but it can cause changes in the bowel and digestive tract. One theory is that the brain sends signals to the stomach which affect how the stomach functions. It's thought that acids and other substances are secreted in response to these signals. Stress can slow down intestinal function, leading to constipation, gassiness, and nausea. At other times stress speeds up intestinal function, causing cramping and diarrhea. Regular exercise releases endorphins, which help relax the abdomen, and this lessens symptoms.

If you feel stressed, quiet yourself, breathe more slowly, and tell yourself, "I'm feeling calm and relaxed." This sends a message to your subconscious mind that can help ease the anxiety. If you find yourself tensing up as you talk, consciously lower your voice a tone or two. This will make you feel calmer, because a high-pitched voice indicates stress. There are herbal remedies that also help manage stress. If all else fails, a doctor may need to prescribe an anti-anxiety drug to help relieve stress and tension.

Meditation is an excellent way of combating stress.

Some may think that they need twenty or thirty minutes to relax, but even five minutes of stillness can be rejuvenating. Sit quietly and breathe deeply several times. Inhale through your nose. Exhale through your mouth. Imagine a white beam of light over your head pouring relaxing and healing energy into the crown center at the top of your head. As this light flows through you, feel the tension drain away through the soles of your feet. End your meditation with several deep breaths.

Feeling lonely or isolated, especially when we're under stress, can increase our chances of getting sick. Having the support of friends and family seems to reduce the risk of illnesses like colds, flu, and perhaps even heart disease and other serious disorders. Friendships also appear to bolster the immune system. Maintaining friendships is as important for our health as exercising and eating the right kinds of food.

Scientists still don't know why people with strong ties to family, friends, colleagues, and the community not only appear to be healthier and to age more slowly but also seem to have a significantly longer average lifespan than isolated, lonely individuals. One theory is that love and friendship act as a buffer against stress, which often takes a devastating toll on the body.

It seems that the number of friends we have is not as important as the quality of that friendship. True friends accept and love us for who we really are. For some, having one true friend who gives love and emotional support may be enough. Having too large a circle of friends may put added demands on our time and energy and may be more a hindrance than a help.

It is good to have a diverse group of people as friends, including family, coworkers, and mate. We may chose both male and female friends, some of whom may be younger and some older than we are. Some friends may be bosom buddies, while other relationships may be more casual. I have discovered that having a friend who is on the same spiritual path is a wonderful blessing. New ideas can be discussed and information from books and articles shared. As we get nearer to our goal of enlightenment, it will be more important than ever to have a friend who understands. I suggest to my clients that if they don't have as many friends as they would like, that they need to get involved in some group of like-minded people. Perhaps they can join a sports or hobby club, or a religious or spiritual group. How can we make new friends? My mother's advice is as true today as it was when I was a child: "If you want to have friends, be friendly."

The best way to lose a friend is to feel sorry for ourselves and dump our problems and complaints on them. When we're centered only on ourselves, we're in serious trouble. We all need to bring to a friendship fresh ideas and opportunities for new adventures. Another way to lose friends is to become overly familiar. It is important that we respect others' privacy and not drop in at a friend's home without phoning ahead to make sure she is available. Even though our friends may be critical of their mates and children, we need to be very careful that we do not criticize them. We not only lose friends but also respect and trust when we are told something in secret and we pass on that private information. Some people feel that a friendship should be an even give-and-take, but we don't have to keep track of who called last or whose turn it is to treat for lunch. Instead, we need to give our time, gifts, and love freely without expecting anything in return.

Some of us are so busy that it's not always easy to find the time or energy to be with our friends; but friendship, like the plants in our garden, needs to be cared for with love. We need to be able to share our joys and sorrows and to give each other moral support in times of crisis. As friends, we don't have to solve others' problems. What they really want is for us be attentive and compassionate listeners. We should not expect our friends to give more time and energy to the friendship than they are able to give. When we have found a good friend, we need to find joy in the positive aspects of the relationship. If the friend says or does something that hurts our feelings, we don't have to dwell on it. A friendship is more important than a few unkind words. We can let the negative times simply flow past without letting them affect us. True friendship exists when we know each other's faults and shortcomings and we are still able to express unconditional love.

Sometimes when a person lives alone, especially if they have few friends or outside interests, having a pet to love is beneficial to both their physical and emotional health. Taking care of a dog, cat, or bird is a wonderful way to alleviate loneliness. Pets respond to love and give generous quantities of affection in return. For many people, a pet can become a best friend.

It's not easy to leave our friends and move to a new area where we don't know anyone. When I retired and moved to Eugene, Oregon, I woke up one morning and said to my Higher Self, "I'm so lonely and depressed. I did what you told me to and moved here. Now I'm living in this little rented house waiting for my home to be built on my ranch and I have nothing to do. I'm lonely and bored. I need to have something to do. I need to meet people who will help fill the emptiness that I am feeling. I need a friend!"

Inside my head, I heard one word: "Volunteer."

So that is exactly what I did. On Monday mornings, I worked at the Red Cross office answering the phone and helping with food distribution. On Tuesday mornings, I picked up a blind man and took him shopping or to his doctor. On Wednesday afternoons, I worked in a local church office answering the phone and typing letters for the minister. On Thursdays, I picked up flowers that were past their prime at several florists and took them to a nursing home. On Fridays, I taught a class on reincarnation at the community college. I was busy and feeling good about myself, and in a short time I had a circle of friends.

Fifteen years have gone by, and although some of the people I met have moved away, the rest are still my good friends. One by one, as I became busier with my counseling and teaching, I let my volunteer jobs go, but they had filled an important role in my life when I really needed to overcome my depression, loneliness, and boredom.

If you, like some of my clients, have retired or find yourself with more time than you know what to do with, my one word to you is *volunteer*. If you decide to be a volunteer, you may find agencies looking for help listed in the front of your telephone book. You may also find out what opportunities are available from your community YMCA, church or synagogue, senior-citizen groups, or community outreach programs. Hospitals always need extra help and often have auxiliaries that organize volunteers. They need people to do everything from holding babies and wheeling patients to their rooms to delivering flowers and doing clerical work.

Think about what you really enjoy doing. Do you like working with children, teens, or the elderly? Maybe you have some particular expertise to offer. Would you like to do something that's different from the way you normally spend your time? For example, if you work alone in a home office, you might want to find a project that puts you in the midst of lots of people. If you work with people, perhaps you would prefer to do some quiet volunteer work in a library.

Be careful that you don't overextend yourself. What kind of time commitment can you realistically make? Can you volunteer two hours a week or two hours each morning? It's unwise to select a project just because you feel that it's the right thing to do. If you choose a job you really don't want, chances are you won't last long. You may continue to do the volunteer work but feel resentful of the time spent in a service you really don't want to be doing. Don't feel guilty if you change your mind and decide to quit a job you have said you would do. There may be just the right volunteer job waiting for you somewhere else. When you volunteer your time and energy, you will discover the happiness and satisfaction of helping others.

Many people go through life believing that their happiness or unhappiness is largely determined by the people and events in their environment. Others feel that their happiness is dependent on whether they have good or bad luck. The truth is that happiness is an *internal* affair. Two people may be in exactly the same circumstances, yet one finds happiness and the other unhappiness. For some people, happiness is tantalizingly just around the corner. However, we need to resist the temptation to postpone our happiness: until vacation time, until our job promotion, until we get married, until we move into our new home, until we retire. Difficulties are a fact of life. As one challenge is overcome, another inevitably appears in its place. The sooner we accept this, the sooner we can stop postponing our happiness until everything is perfect. We need to accept the fact that the challenges we have chosen to experience are an important part of our unique spiritual journey through life. Try counting your blessings and successes rather than dwelling on your losses and failures. Remember, happiness is an inside job.

As a counselor, I've learned the true meaning of compassion. It is a deep feeling of sympathy and empathy for the suffering or misfortune of others. As much as we might like to alleviate their emotional pain, we can't save them from the condition that they have created for themselves. All people are totally responsible for everything that happens to them. Thus, the pain is their choice, and only they can choose not to experience it. The degree of our compassion depends not only on how much we care about people, but also on how willing they are to accept responsibility for their situation and then do something about it. As a counselor, I cannot solve my clients' problems for them, but I can point out the options that are available to them and encourage them to rise above their difficulties. I can have compassion for them, but it's up to them to learn the lessons that they have chosen to learn from this experience. A difficult situation can be a time for growth, and in that growth it is possible to discover the true self.

One of the special gifts that come to us when we become enlightened is an inner peace. This is a peace that is beyond human understanding. It is having peace within our Soul even when we are in the midst of turmoil and disaster. It is knowing that we are one with our Higher Self, our partner in life's big adventure. In order to have this inner peace, we need to constantly have peace of mind as our goal. Inner peace is experienced as we learn to forgive the world and everyone in it. From a peace-filled mind arises a peaceful perception of the world. World peace begins with each one of us as we become filled with peace.

As a child, I learned that God is love. That is still the most profound definition of God that can be given. Love is the most powerful motivating force in the universe. The great outpouring of God's love is continually being offered to all. God's love flows to our Higher Self who, in turn, sends it to us through our crown center as a stream of energy. As we become enlightened, we will be completely filled with love all the time, and our supply will always be full and running over. By giving our love away to others, we actually increase the love within ourselves.

Every human being is hungry for love, so it is the one perfect gift that we can give to others. We need to give this gift without the faintest expectation of receiving something in return — without hope of reward, compensation, or even appreciation. We need to give love to the person standing behind us in the check-out line or sitting next to us on the bus. We need to give love to our friends and family, plus a double portion to our enemies, because they need it more than any of the others. Love washes away all hate, discord, confusion, and imperfection. The greater our love, the greater the blessing it will carry. No words need to be spoken as we send forth our love from our heart center. If we wish, we can visualize a stream of peach-colored energy going from our heart to the other person's heart. (I use peach instead of pink because pink can be mistaken for a sexual attraction.) As love flows out of us, it brings healing first to us and then to those around us.

As parents, we need to teach our children love until it is a natural part of their lives. We also need to teach them to see people's strength rather than their weakness, to give love to those who seem unlovable, and to see the beauty and the love in the world around them. By our example, they will learn to love. As they return our love, we will have taught them the greatest lesson in all the world.

When we love life despite its problems and difficulties, we can prevent damaging changes in body chemistry and counter the harmful effects of such negative emotions as fear or hatred. Negative emotions affect not only the emotional body, but also the physical and energy bodies. Positive emotions, such as faith, hope, and love, also affect all of our bodies and not only dispel the negative emotions but also provide a buffer against the day-to-day stress that can weaken our immunity, increase cholesterol, and elevate blood pressure.

Our lives will always include challenges, anxieties, and frustrations. The truth is that life doesn't always have a fairy-tale, happy ending. Even if all our problems can't be solved in the way we had hoped, we can begin to understand and accept that everything in life offers us an opportunity to learn a lesson. Learning to balance our emotional body and to rise above our problems with a sense of serenity and inner peace brings us closer to our goal of enlightenment.

4

Understanding the Power of the Mind

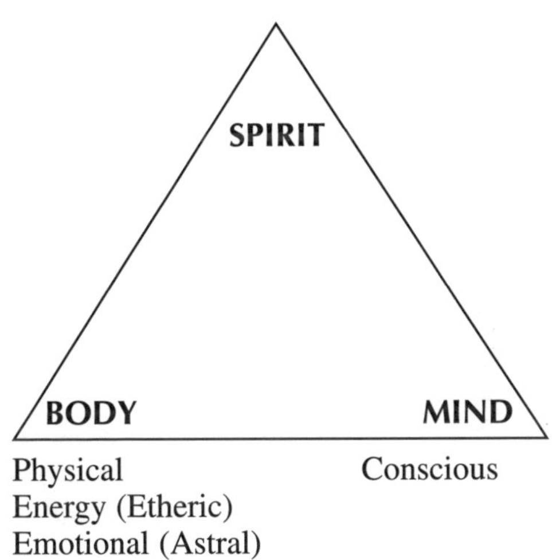

Physical
Energy (Etheric)
Emotional (Astral)

Conscious

Throughout the ages, philosophers, scientists and others have pondered the mysteries of the mind. They have attempted to explain the mind and its relationship to the brain. The brain is made of physical material. It can be weighed, dissected, and analyzed. The mind, on the other hand, is energy and spirit. It cannot be seen nor can it be analyzed under a microscope, but we can begin to discover how the mind works. Our mind is an important power in our life, the producer of our thoughts. Our thoughts in turn create our personal reality. Neuroscientists believe that thoughts, feelings, dreams, and other brain activities are produced by chemical and electrical impulses in the network of nerve cells that make up most of the brain. We may not understand exactly how our mind works, but we can begin to realize the tremendous power of our thoughts. The power of the mind has the potential to bring happiness, health, and contentment into our lives.

Our thoughts are what make us different from every other person in the world. Thoughts make some people rich, others poor; some people healthy, others sick; some people happy, others sad. We can never get away from our own thoughts. When our thoughts dwell on negative things, we get negative results. Likewise, when our thoughts are flowing in a positive manner, the results will be positive.

We have four different types of consciousness. Besides the conscious mind, we have the unconscious, the subconscious, and the superconscious minds. All work together, but each also has specific characteristics. The conscious mind is that part concerned primarily with logical, rational, conceptual thought. It is the active aspect of the mind. The conscious mind picks up knowledge received through our five senses. Every thought that enters the conscious mind is either accepted or rejected. If we accept a thought or idea as true, it is stored in the subconscious mind, which retains it for future use. Our subconscious mind records our thoughts and emotions and stores them away as memories. Our unconscious mind regulates the autonomic nervous system which operates the bodily functions that must go on constantly even while we are sleeping or unconscious. Finally, our superconscious mind connects us with our Higher Self.

Doctors and scientists are now able to explore some of the mysteries of the mind with the help of information gained from an electroencephalograph. Whether we are wide awake, meditating, or sound asleep, our billions of brain cells give off small waves of electricity. The chemical generators that produce and control these brain waves are located in the nerve cells of the brain. To detect brain waves, doctors attach electrodes onto a person's head by using a special paste to ensure contact with the scalp. Then electrically driven pens record the waves on a continuously moving strip of paper. This record is called an "electroencephalogram" or "EEG." When we are actively using our conscious mind to solve problems or in other mental activities, our brain produces fast, low-voltage brain waves called "beta waves," which range from thirteen cycles to as high as forty cycles per second. When we are meditating or on the borderline between consciousness and the sleep state, the brain produces alpha waves, which range from eight to thirteen cycles per second. In deep sleep, the delta brain waves are even slower, occurring four to seven cycles per second.

When the brain's nerve centers are upset, the tracings of the brain waves are jagged and uneven. This enables doctors to diagnose epilepsy and to locate brain tumors. Abnormal brain waves can also result from head injuries, infections of the brain, or lack of oxygen.

Because our thoughts produce brain waves, it is possible to communicate our thoughts to another person without the use of our five senses. Thought transference or telepathy involves information sent from one person to another through a type of mind contact.

To better understand brain waves, let us consider how sound waves are produced. When we speak, we are forcing air past our vocal cords, causing them to vibrate, and this produces sound waves. These vibrations travel through the air until they reach a person's ear. When the sound waves make contact with the eardrum, it begins to vibrate. The sound waves are turned into nerve impulses inside the cochlea tube, and then the nerves send the information to the brain.

As we think, we produce brain waves that correspond to our thought patterns. These electromagnetic waves travel through space at the speed of light. The waves produce vibrations which can be picked up by another person through sensitive nerve cells in the skin, especially in the brow area. The waves are then directed to the pineal gland, which is the center for the inner ear. There the vibrations are changed into nerve impulses and the message is relayed to the conscious mind.

It is believed that our earliest ancestors were more telepathic than we are in modern times. They could communicate with each other by sending their thoughts over long distances. As time passed, people learned to shield their minds. By keeping their thoughts and intentions to themselves, people were more likely to survive and have children who could also keep their thoughts private. It is believed that the number of people with mind shields increased until most human beings were able to keep their thoughts secret from others. Telepathy still took place, but only when thoughts were purposely transmitted to someone. The good news is that we inherited from our ancestors the ability to shield our private thoughts from public scrutiny. The bad news is that most of us have forgotten how to communicate telepathically with each other.

If we want to communicate telepathically, we will need to learn the art of telepathy. It seems that some people are naturally better receivers and some are better senders. Usually someone who talks a lot and has an active mind makes the best sender, while a person with a mind that is receptive and relaxed is the best receiver. A good time to practice telepathy is in the early morning when the atmosphere is the calmest and the mind is more relaxed. Decide beforehand how much time you and your partner will need for the experiment. Enter the alpha state by closing your eyes and becoming completely relaxed. If you are the receiver, quiet your mind and become receptive to the message being sent. The receiver should record all the impressions that are mentally obtained in the time allotted for the experiment. The sender needs to send out a strong, concentrated message. The stronger the thought, the better the chance it has of reaching the other person. Distance does not seem to affect the power of telepathy. The sender can be in an adjoining room or in another state. During one of our moon landings, two scientists — one on Earth and one on the moon — performed experiments using telepathy to communicate with each other.

Spontaneous telepathy often occurs when impressions are sent during times of crisis from someone who is in an emotionally charged situation. Ordinary, everyday telepathic impressions occur more often than most of us realize. They significantly influence our emotions and behavior whether we are aware of it or not. This is especially true between people living or working closely together. There are some people who seem to be *on the same wave length*. Without even being aware, they may be receiving telepathic impressions from someone close to them.

We are all able to send out thoughts that can be received by others; thus, we continually affect others by these waves of thought. Public opinion is largely created in this way. Many people think along certain lines, not because they have carefully thought out an idea and come to a conclusion, but because they are being influenced by the thoughts of others. A strong leader's words go out over the airways via the radio and television and are received by receptive minds. These people, in turn, affect still more people with their thoughts. In this way, public opinion can be created by the thoughts of a few people influencing the minds of a large majority.

Just as there may be times when our physical body becomes ill, we may also experience mental illness. A mental illness is really no different than a physical illness, yet until recently a stigma has been attached to mental illness. None of us is immune to experiencing mental illness. It touches the lives of people in all walks of life, regardless of age, race, education, or income. Mental illness affects a person's ability to think clearly, to act appropriately, and to relate to others in a positive manner.

Doctors classify mental illnesses in two ways. *Organic* illness results from defects that occur in the brain before birth, or when injury or illness causes damage to the brain. Most mental illnesses, however, are *functional*, in that there is no apparent physical change in the brain but the mind does not work properly. Even though the symptoms may seem to be only mental in nature, no illness is entirely mental, just as no disease is entirely physical. Like physical illnesses, most functional mental disorders can be treated effectively with medication.

Scientists have discovered that many people suffering from mental illnesses have an imbalance in the way their brain metabolizes certain chemicals called "neurotransmitters." Too much or too little of these chemicals may result in depression, anxiety, or other emotional or mental disorders. Medicines have been developed that can alter the way in which the brain produces, stores, and releases neurotransmitter chemicals, thereby alleviating the symptoms of some mental illnesses. Most doctors recognize that many factors contribute to our mental health and that it is important to take into consideration all these factors when treating their patients.

Our mind can be compared to a motion-picture projector sending our thoughts out into the world. If our state of mind is one of contentment and peace, that is what we will project, and therefore our world and the people in it will appear to be at peace. On the other hand, if our mind is filled with upsetting thoughts, we will project this state outward, and we will see our world and those in it as upsetting to us. Our mind is also the director, producer, scriptwriter, film editor, and critic of our life story. Not only does our mind have the power of making all decisions, it also has the capability of changing our life story at any time. It is important that we recognize the creative power of our thoughts, a power far greater than most of us can comprehend.

Negative, evil thoughts have as much power as positive, good thoughts — and, in some cases, even more. However, there is available to us a powerful protection from any negativity. Just as the White Light, the essence of God, coming through our Higher Self can bring to us healing energy, it can also provide us with a protective shield. Whenever we find ourselves in a situation where negativity is prevalent, we need to ask our Higher Self for this protection. If we are living or working with negatively thinking people, we can use this White Light as a cloak surrounding our emotional body. This is especially important if we are working with children, the elderly, or people who are physically or mentally ill. It is possible for them to drain us psychically of our energy if we are not protected by the White Light.

Angry, hateful thoughts are capable of traveling to the person involved and can negatively affect the emotional body. If that person, however, has asked to be encircled with the White Light, these negative thoughts will bounce off this shield and will return to the sender.

After a heated argument, negative thought forms

hang in the room where the confrontation took place. Psychically these thought forms appear as dirty gray clouds hovering near the ceiling. It's as important to give our home a spiritual cleansing as it is a physical cleaning. We can do this by going into each room and asking our Higher Self to fill it with White Light. No two physical objects can occupy the same space at the same time. This is also true of spirit objects. When the White Light fills the room, no negativity can remain. When renting or buying a house, it is important that we give the place a thorough spiritual cleansing to get rid of any lingering negative thought forms. Even when we are traveling, it is wise to give our hotel or motel room a spiritual cleaning.

Negative, manmade thought forms have created the concept of a devil. These thought forms are based on fear and are used to control people. If an individual or a group of people needs fear to keep others in line, they can create a very real devil. However, the devil exists only because they give it power.

"Voodoo" is the name given to the religious beliefs and practices of certain African tribes. These beliefs and practices have spread to the West Indies and to some parts of the United States. Sometimes very powerful negative thought forms are used to create Voodoo magic. It is believed that someone can harm or kill an enemy by making an image of the person and sticking pins into it. Cases have been reported involving people who have become ill or even died because they believed that they were the subject of a Voodoo curse.

Last year a deeply disturbed young couple, José and Maria, came to me for counseling. They told me that a man they thought was their friend had become their enemy because he felt cheated in a business transaction. The man was so angry that he confronted José and told him that he had paid someone to cast an evil spell upon the couple. I explained to José and Maria how they could protect themselves from all harm by asking their Higher Self to surround them with White Light. I also explained that no evil could penetrate this shield of protection. When Maria came for an appointment several months later, I was deeply saddened to hear that the stress of the evil spell hanging over José had been too great. Her husband had committed suicide. José believed that his enemy was *out to get him*, so it really didn't matter whether or not there was an evil spell. It seems difficult to understand how anyone in this day and age could be so negatively influenced. Since her husband's suicide, Maria has gotten her life together, sold their home, and moved to another state.

In a way, you and I are being bombarded with *evil spells* right in our living rooms — through television. They are now running a commercial stating that the flu season is upon us and that it will be worse this year than it was last year. To reinforce this idea, they show someone *suffering* from the flu. These ads and others like them are filling our homes with negative thought forms. If we go to sleep while the television is on, our subconscious mind is still recording what is being said. It is wise for us to feed only positive thoughts into our subconscious mind. When I am watching television, I put it on mute during commercials. I also change to another channel if what I am watching is presenting a negative impression.

We create our own reality by our thoughts and actions, therefore, we are responsible for the environment in which we live. We are also the creators of our personal Heaven or Hell. Neither Heaven nor Hell is a specific place, but rather they are states of consciousness. There are some who believe that Heaven is a far off place where we will go when we die if we have the right religious beliefs or if we are good enough. They also believe that those who are not good enough will end up in an eternal Hell. It is true that the lower planes of the Astral World are bleak, dreary, and devoid of love. It is also true that the higher planes of the Astral World are filled with love, peace, and beauty. But the truth is that Heaven can be within each of us right now. We are creating Heaven or Hell every day of our lives by our thoughts and actions.

When we are in a heavenly state of consciousness, we know that we are one with our Higher Self, the God essence within each of us. We have a feeling of inner peace and contentment, and we are consciously aware that we are divinely protected and greatly loved. Hell, on the other hand, is the feeling of being separated from God. It is being filled with negativity — hate, guilt, fear, anger, or revenge. It is a feeling of not being worthy of the good that God wants to shower upon us. When we understand the Truth about heaven and hell, we can begin creating our own Heaven right here on Earth. This is a necessary step towards our achieving enlightenment.

Everything is first an idea. Then comes a mental picture of that idea. Imagination is the ability to create an idea or mental picture in our mind. Creative visualization is magic in the truest sense of the word. It involves understanding the natural principles that govern the workings of the mind and learning how to use these principles in the proper way. Imagination, when rightly used, is a very special gift. The mental images that we consciously accept as true are impressed on the subconscious mind and will indeed manifest in our lives.

In creative visualization, we are able to use our imagination to create a clear image of something we wish to manifest. We might imagine a new car, a better job, or a new relationship. After relaxing into a quiet meditative state, we can create a mental picture of what we desire. At first, we will probably need to do our visualization several times a day. If we are sincere in our desire and intention, we will actually achieve what we have visualized.

If clients find it difficult to visualize, I suggest to them, "You can make a *treasure map*. On a heavy paper, paste pictures that represent what you are *wishing for*. Hang the treasure map where you can see it during the day. Think about your goal and then picture yourself receiving that which you desire. Whether you use visualization or a treasure map, what you are doing is sending a request to your Higher Self saying, *I really desire this in my life*. But be sure this is something that will benefit both you and those around you."

If we don't succeed in getting what we want, it may be because we do not have the patience to stick to one idea long enough to see it through. Perhaps we give up too easily, or we keep changing our minds because we are not really sure of what we do want. It may take more time and patience than we thought to make our dreams come true. Another reason we may not be getting what we want is because our thoughts are not real enough. When we create an image in our mind it must be clear and well visualized if it is to be strong enough to become a reality.

We can control and direct our imagination constructively and get what we want in life, or we can use it negatively and imagine what we don't want. The mental images that we contemplate and consciously accept as true are impressed on our subconscious mind. If we feel a lack of prosperity, we need to realize that lack exists because we have chosen those particular thoughts. We are literally attracting to ourselves exactly what we are thinking. Therefore, lack of abundance results when we have chosen the thoughts that are attracting to us a poverty consciousness. Rather than working so hard against poverty or against not having enough, we can relax and allow abundance to flow to us.

When we worry, we are using visualization in a negative manner. Worry means we are anxious about something that has not yet happened. When we worry, we are focusing our attention on a condition, experience, or event which disturbs us and which we don't want to happen. Often, we repeat the same train of thought over and over again without reaching any solution. To overcome worry, we need to consciously substitute positive, constructive thoughts for our negative, worrisome thoughts. When a negative thought enters the mind, it is better not to fight with it directly but to utilize the fact that the mind can only think of one thing at a time. As we concentrate on positive thoughts, the negative thoughts will be forced from our mind. It is important that we think of what we desire to receive and refuse to think of what we do not want to bring into our lives.

Through visualization, we can use the power of our mind to ease our pain and to heal our physical body. To make this work, we need to believe in the power of our imagination. We also need to be able to concentrate and focus on the pictures that we produce in our minds. In a quiet, comfortable environment, we can close our eyes, relax the whole body, and enter the alpha state. We may choose to listen to a special tape that will help us achieve an altered state of consciousness. Now we are ready to see pictures on the screen of the mind.

Visualization works best when we come up with our own mental images. Here are a few suggestions to show how visualization works in healing the body and easing pain. If you have a stomach-ache, you might imagine there is a ball of fire in your stomach. Then visualize a stream of water completely extinguishing the fire, leaving you feeling cool and refreshed. For a backache, visualize the pain as a long sword driven deep into your spine; now picture the sword being slowly pulled out, removing the pain and leaving no trace of the wound. For a blocked sinus, imagine a stopped-up sink, then visualize the drain being unclogged, allowing the water to flow freely down the drain. A cancer patient might envision a knight in shining armor using his lance to stab and kill the enemy tumor cells. A friend of mine who has survived breast cancer told me that she believes she owes her recovery to positive thoughts, meditation, and imaging. In her visualization, she saw a black crow devouring the cancer cells one at a time until they were all gone. These are some examples of visualization that may help you create your own personal mental image.

We should not try to hurry our visualization session. We need to take enough time to produce a vivid, complete thought form in our mind. At first we may need to use visualization several times a day until we experience an improvement in our physical or emotional health; however, sometimes a single session may bring relief. By using this simple technique of relaxation and visualization, we have within our power the ability to heal both our physical and emotional bodies. Visualization, however, needs to be used in conjunction with Western medicine and alternative methods of healing.

Visualization helps us to acquire the material things that we desire. We cannot possess anything without first thinking about it. If we want to build a new home, or buy or rent a house that is already built, we need to visualize that home in our imagination. Our mental picture should be specific and in detail. If we are looking for a house to rent or buy, once we have a definite image in our mind, we will need to contact a realtor. If we are planning to build a new home, we will need to hire a contractor. Then we will be able to work closely with him as he draws up the blueprints for our dream house.

Those of you who know me personally are aware that my home is a product of my visualization. Before I moved to Eugene, I spent many months planning every aspect of the house I planned to build, down to the smallest detail. I drew complete blueprints and pictured each room, inside and out. It's a joy for me to be able to live in the home of my dreams. It's a beautiful cedar house with large windows overlooking a forest of fir and cedar and a giant old oak tree. With twenty-six acres of land, there is not another house in sight. Every morning when I get up and see the deer grazing in the meadow, I give thanks for the peace and beauty that surround me

Several years ago, I decided that I would really love to buy a gold station wagon at a price that would be right for me. I visualized a station wagon with room enough for my six grandchildren. Imagine my surprise when the first car I saw at the Ford dealership was the exact one I had pictured in my mind. It was a beautiful seven-passenger gold Taurus station wagon. It was only a year old and had low mileage. Being a practical person, I went to four other car dealerships that day, but I came back and purchased the first car that I had seen at the price I could afford. I firmly believe in the power of visualization; however, I didn't expect to sit back and wait for someone to deliver a station wagon to my home. It was my responsibility to go out and find my car and pay for it myself.

It takes patience and perseverance along with the power of the mind to get results. When I moved into my new home, I began to visualize a marble coffee table to put in front of my divan. When I phoned the various furniture stores in the area, none of them had even heard of a marble coffee table. Time passed, but I kept the image of the table in my mind. One day I saw in the display window of a furniture store two marble end tables. I went inside the store and asked a salesman if they had a marble coffee table. The salesman told me that he hadn't seen one, but he would go into the warehouse and find out if they had received one. There, still in its wooden crate and newly shipped from Italy, was a marble coffee table. It took awhile, but my visualization had finally become a reality.

Visualization is useful if you wish to sell something. Doris, one of my close friends, phoned to cancel our date to have Sunday brunch together. She told me that she and her husband had decided to change one of their bedrooms into an office, so she had advertised her bedroom set for sale in the newspaper. This was the last day the ad would run and she still hadn't sold the furniture. I reminded Doris of the power of visualization and suggested that she picture a person coming to her door with money in hand, eager to buy the bedroom set. Only a couple of hours later, Doris called to tell me that a young woman had purchased the furniture because the bedroom set was exactly what she wanted. When you plan to sell something, be sure that the price is a fair one, that you really want to sell the item, and that you put the power of your mind into the transaction through visualization.

The parents of my friend Lana had decided to sell their home and buy a smaller place after all their children had moved out. Their home had been on the market for almost a year and it still hadn't sold. Lana told me that they had a good realtor, and the price was in line with other houses on the block that had recently sold. The landscaping was professionally manicured, and the house was immaculate both inside and outside. Lana asked me what I thought was blocking the sale of the house. I asked Lana if both her parents really wanted to sell their home and move to a smaller house. When Lana thought about my question, she realized that her father didn't want to move: obviously, the power of his mind was holding up the sale. Lana's parents finally decided to take their house off the market because they both agreed that they loved their beautiful home and didn't really want to move.

Because we have free will, we can think any thoughts that we wish. We can think that we are important and intelligent, or we can think that we are stupid and not worth very much. We can think that others are out to exploit, hurt, or reject us, or we can believe that people will be nice to us, treat us fairly, and be there if we need their help. We also create our own moods and emotions. We can feel sad by dwelling on the tragic times in our life, or we can feel happy by remembering the good things that have happened to us. We can create our own personal devil to frighten us, or we can surround ourselves with the love of our Higher Self. We can become fearful when we imagine that something bad is going to happen to us, or we can have faith that we will attract that which is good into our lives.

Now is the time to accept the fact that you are in control of your own life, and that through your thoughts you create your personal reality. Only then will you be able to understand the tremendous power of your mind.

5

Programming
the Subconscious Mind

The subconscious mind is like a computer recording not only all that we see, hear, and feel, but also our thoughts and emotions. The conscious mind picks up knowledge from outside sources and passes it inward to the subconscious mind, where it is retained as a memory. The subconscious does not reason or judge but stores everything the conscious mind sends it. So we need to be careful that we feed only positive thoughts and emotions into our personal computer.

We not only program our subconscious mind, but in a way our subconscious programs us. The subconscious mind works to create the reality for which it has been programmed. Perhaps we experienced a fearful but forgotten trauma as a child. This resulted in negative programming of the subconscious. The childhood experience may not relate to us today, yet when faced with a similar situation, we may experience irrational anxiety. The information that has been programmed into our personal computer as the result of our past experiences largely determines who we are today.

Everything that we see is programmed into the subconscious mind. Sometimes we make mistakes in interpreting the impressions our eyes perceive. In the case of an optical illusion, things are not always the way they seem to be. Things that are closer to us only appear to be larger than those farther away. When we look into a mirror, the reflection we see is the result of information we have programmed into our subconscious mind. People who suffer from anorexia are so emaciated that they look like their skin is stretched over the skeleton, yet they have such a distorted body image that when they look into a mirror they think they look fat. When you or I look into a mirror, we need to ignore our flaws and see our true beauty reflected back to us.

There may be times when we observe something that we are not even consciously aware of seeing. Chris was standing on a street corner waiting for the light to change when a car went through a red light, hit another car, and sped off, leaving a young woman with massive head injuries. When the police arrived, Chris told them what he had seen, but he couldn't remember the exact make or color of the car because it had all happened so quickly. Chris agreed to go down to the police station and be hypnotized to see if he could remember more details. Under hypnosis, Chris remembered not only the make and color of the car but also the license plate number. Even though

Chris was not consciously aware of this information, it had been stored in his subconscious mind. With Chris's help, the police were able to arrest the hit-and-run driver.

There are some people who go through life with their eyes half-closed, forming few if any visual images. Others are a little more observant, while still others have become adept at accurate observation. What we consciously observe will make a difference in how we see life. Two people look out a window; one sees the gray skies, while the other sees the magic of dewdrops on a spider's web. We choose where we want to direct our attention and, thus, what we program into the subconscious mind. We can concentrate on the part of our world that is ugly, or we can enjoy the beauty that surrounds us.

What we hear is also stored in the subconscious mind. However, our hearing sometimes plays tricks on us. What was said and what we think was said may not be the same. At other times, we hear only what we want to hear and filter out the rest. Everyone thought my father-in-law, Nye, was profoundly deaf, but still he wouldn't buy a hearing aid. His wife, Margaret, finally gave up trying to talk to Nye because he didn't hear her even when she yelled. Yet Nye and I could carry on a normal conversation together. He had just stopped listening to his talkative, nagging wife. Many teenagers have become quite adept at tuning out their parents and teachers. Sometimes the words we hear are misunderstood because of the inflection in a person's voice. When someone says, "You look nice today," we normally accept it as a compliment. However, some might think of it as a put-down. They might feel that the person was really saying, "Usually you don't look nice, but today you do." Our subconscious mind records what we think we have heard from our point of view.

Because our subconscious mind cannot differentiate

between reality and fantasy, we can play a game I call "Acting As If." As I began writing this chapter, I came down with bronchitis, a bacterial infection. I had a wheezing and rattling in my chest and a body-shaking cough. Usually I'm a very healthy person, so this gave me an opportunity to practice what I preach. I needed to put on an act for my subconscious mind to keep from registering my illness. When I got up each morning, I dressed, combed my hair, and put on some makeup. Then when I looked into the mirror, at least I didn't look like death warmed over. I shifted into survival mode. The dishes could pile up in the sink and the dust could settle on the furniture. My priorities were to feel as comfortable as possible and to get well, the sooner the better. When my friends and family phoned to ask how I was feeling, my reply was, "I'm getting better." I said it loud and clear so my subconscious mind would hear and record this information. When we act as if we are feeling better, our bodies respond by actually helping us to feel better.

The Acting As If game can work in other aspects of our life as well. If we are sad, we can put on a happy face and act as if we are happy. When we lack courage, we can act as if we are brave. If we have low self-esteem, we can act as if we are confident. It's amazing how the subconscious mind will help us become winners.

We can program our subconscious to use the power of the mind in a positive, optimistic way or in a negative, pessimistic way. Life doesn't make us feel bad — our thinking does. We would never set out to intentionally hurt ourselves by our thoughts. However, it seems that negative thinking is an attempt to convince ourselves that feeling bad is really justified. In fact, pessimists will usually be able to point to a reason why they feel so negative. It is important to realize, however, that the events we think are causing the negativity usually aren't the problem after all.

In college I had a roommate, Judy, whose life sounded like a soap opera in reruns. Over and over she would relate how she had been mistreated as a child ... how her sister had gotten all the new clothes plus the love and attention from the rest of the family ... how she wasn't as smart or as beautiful as her sister. Whether or not it was true really wasn't the point. She had replayed these tapes so often that she had programmed her subconscious mind to believe it was true. Judy had brought with her such a feeling of inferiority that it kept her from achieving her full potential in college. She was a victim of her own negative thinking.

Some people, like Judy, are stuck in their negative subconscious thought patterns. No one really wants to have negative thoughts such as "Life isn't worth living." However, these and other negative thoughts sometimes become a familiar pattern and just seem to appear in the mind. After all, things may not be going well and negative thinking may seem justified. Eventually negative reinforcement convinces us further that we were right: "Life isn't worth living."

Some people see their problems as problems! They whine and worry and verbalize them over and over. The more they repeat them the more they program this negativity into the subconscious mind. Others, however, see their problems as opportunities and challenges. They learn from these challenges and turn them into opportunities. Thus, the resulting computer programming is positive. The only difference between problem-oriented people and opportunity-oriented people is attitude. This makes all the difference! If we see our problems as opportunities, we will no longer have any problems.

Negative thinking often creeps into our minds insidiously and gets us nowhere. The more willingly we go along with our negative thoughts, the worse we will feel. We cannot withstand the negative influence of self-defeating thinking for very long. Eventually we must either reprogram the subconscious mind to think more positively or face the results of pessimistic thinking — self-pity, unhappiness, and depression.

If we have programmed the subconscious mind to see life in a pessimistic way, we are just as capable of changing the way we look at life once we make the commitment to do so. Anyone can learn the art of optimism. First, we need to understand that our thoughts originate within us — that we create them. Second, if we have the habit of thinking negatively, we need to recognize and acknowledge it. It's true that some people seem to be natural optimists, but most of us have to learn how to be optimistic. In order to change our outlook on life from pessimistic to optimistic, it is necessary to reprogram the subconscious mind. Habits are not easy to break. This is especially true when dealing with the habit of negative thinking. If we are accustomed to thinking about things in a pessimistic way, we have probably reinforced our negative thinking hundreds of times.

Deciding to reprogram the subconscious mind and to think more positively is an extremely important decision — a life-changing decision. It takes honesty and courage to change. If we have been thinking negatively, we must be honest enough to admit it and courageous enough to change the way we think. Because we are human, negative thoughts will continue to enter the mind, but now we don't have to dwell on these thoughts. We can replace them with positive thoughts. Because we create our thoughts, we open the door to new options. Instead of saying "Nothing ever goes smoothly for me," we can say "Things go smoothly for me most of the time." Instead of thinking "I always make mistakes," or "I'm not smart enough to accomplish this project," we can think "With the help of my partner, my Higher Self, I can do anything I decide to do."

As I tell my students, "A pessimist sees life as he fears it to be. A realist sees life as he believes it to be. An optimist sees life as he hopes it will be. Each moment of each day, you choose to be either pessimistic or optimistic. When you reprogram your subconscious mind from negative to positive thinking, you will create for yourself a little bit of Heaven down here on Earth."

There are many advantages in approaching life with an optimistic attitude. A recent study showed that, in general, optimists are healthier than pessimists. Optimists are more likely to try to maintain their health by getting regular physical check-ups and by taking their medicine as directed. After surgery, doctors have found, optimists usually recover sooner and are able to resume their normal lives more quickly. Not only does optimism strengthen the immune system, but in a disease like cancer it might mean the difference between living and dying. Optimists usually seek the best treatment and will aggressively fight the disease in a positive manner. A positive attitude also seems to have a protective, healing effect whenever we are exposed to stress, injury, or disease. If we think we are going to be better, we probably will get better.

When we are optimistic, we will use our mind power in a positive way. We will believe in ourselves and, therefore, we will be more likely to achieve our goals. If we think we can reach a goal, we will resist temptation longer. We can tell ourselves, "I can do this. I'm stronger than that piece of chocolate or that cigarette. I know I can do this." An optimistic attitude is an important step in developing a life filled with happiness and contentment. It is also an important step toward achieving enlightenment.

The subconscious mind has no sense of humor. That is why it is important that we are careful about what we say in jest. If we say, "My boss is a pain in the neck," or, "My kids are driving me crazy," our subconscious takes it literally. My suggestion is to use an expression like, "My kids are driving me up a wall." Then visualize yourself with suction boots walking up the wall. By the time you get to the ceiling, you will probably see the humor in the situation and be more relaxed.

Our subconscious mind stores data from the time of our birth until we die. As children, we relied on other people's ideas and beliefs. Our subconscious mind accepted our parents' and teachers' concept of what is right and what is wrong … what is false and what is true. As we grew older, we may have discovered that some of the data that we picked up from adults was incorrect. We realized that we needed to reprogram our subconscious mind. Perhaps your mother told you every time it rained, "You'll catch cold if you get your feet wet." Now as an adult, you want to remove this thought from your memory bank. Repeat over and over, "My body is healthy. I can walk barefoot in the rain and remain healthy." Reprogramming is a much harder task than initial programming, but it is well worth the effort to rid the computer's memory bank of unwanted misinformation.

Our self-esteem develops from a complex interaction of messages passed on to us by our parents and society and programmed into the subconscious mind. These messages become an internal voice that determines how we feel about ourselves. Self-esteem can't be measured on any scale because it is different things to different people. We may feel low self-esteem when our parents and those around us aren't able to give us the love, approval, or acceptance we are looking for. Still we persist. We think that if we say or do the right thing we'll finally get the attention and affection we crave. When that doesn't work, we blame ourselves, not realizing that some people are incapable of giving us the love and recognition we desire. If we carry the hurts of childhood into adult life, they can nag and irritate us and make us doubt ourselves. The negative memories of childhood and the relationships with our parents that contributed to our low self-esteem may be the hardest to reprogram in the subconscious mind.

The most effective way to deal with a poor self-image is to focus on our positive accomplishments. The tendency to judge ourselves harshly often arises from trying to achieve perfection. When our standards are unrealistically high, we either wear ourselves out trying to achieve them or we give up in defeat. Either way we're short-changing ourselves. We often take our achievements for granted and punish ourselves for our failures, both real and imagined. We need to remember our accomplishments with pride and acknowledge a job well done. As we gain confidence in ourselves, we will convey the message that our happiness and fulfillment do not depend on anyone else's acceptance or approval.

Sometimes low self-esteem results when we believe that fate is working against us. We feel that we are victims, and our response is to grow worried and fearful. We give these negative emotions power over us. We need to stop blaming circumstances and instead begin to focus on the causes of our negative emotions.

When we say or do things that indicate a lack of self-respect, the message goes out loud and clear to those around us: "It's okay to walk all over me." But when we say and do things that indicate that we like ourselves, we announce to the world, "I am a worthwhile person and I deserve to be treated well." People usually respond accordingly.

High self-esteem is the feeling that we are valuable, important people. This gives us the resilience to bounce back from life's large and small failures. When we believe in ourselves, we can reprogram our subconscious mind, replacing the negativity of a low self-image with the positive knowledge that we are Masters in the making. More and more, as we realize that we are partners with our Higher Self, we can claim the high self-esteem that is our birthright.

Our parents were probably the ones who were most influential in programming our subconscious minds in our attitude toward money. That may explain why some people with a great deal of money do not feel prosperous, while others with far less money may consider themselves quite well off. Prosperity actually means good fortune and success. It is the satisfaction of feeling secure, fulfilled, and loved. There is a never-ending supply of abundance in the universe, and it belongs to each and every one of us. Abundance is a daily reality which we can create whenever we need it. Of course, a large amount of money may help us to feel even more prosperous. But it is only when we have the feeling of prosperity within us that we will be able to generate and use money for its highest purpose in our lives and in the lives of others.

Clients often come to me asking for advice about money problems. Being human, they yearn for more abundance. I'm sure that most of us would pick prosperity over poverty if given a choice. We may even experience a feeling of frustration or deprivation until we realize that abundance is already ours. Prosperity is often confused with money; however, it is really a state of consciousness. We do not need more money in order to feel prosperous.

Whether we feel prosperous or poor does not depend on the amount of money we have in the bank. It does depend on what our subconscious has been programmed to believe about wealth.

One way to program or reprogram the subconscious mind is by using an affirmation. An affirmation is a short positive statement. By repeating an affirmation, we can change our thoughts, and this in turn can change our personal reality. Each morning as I was growing up, I would hear my dad at the breakfast table state, "Every day, in every way, I am getting better and better." Day after day he filled his subconscious mind with these powerful words, which were self-fulfilling. My father was still mentally alert and physically active when he died as the result of a fall from a ladder at the age of ninety-three.

Using affirmations to change your life is a simple process. Pick an area of your life that needs changing. It can involve a relationship, your health, work, finances, peace of mind, or something else. Decide what you want to change in that area of your life. Using the first person pronoun "I," formulate a concise statement that expresses the desired outcome. Write your affirmation in the present tense, as if the experience were happening in this moment. You could say "I am peaceful" instead of "I will become filled with peace." State your affirmation positively. If you say "I am not angry," the subconscious mind may screen out the "not" and hear only the word "angry." Rephrase the affirmation to directly state what you want — for example, "I now release my resentment." Once you have written your affirmation, say it to yourself a few times. When you have found a good affirmation, it will feel right to you. Sometimes you may need to fine-tune it by altering one or two words. "I am experiencing peace" may work better if stated as "I am at peace," or simply "Peace."

Repeat your affirmation throughout the day. Say it to yourself, or say it out loud. When you repeat an affirmation, you not only program your subconscious mind but you also send the message to your Higher Self. The more you use your affirmation, the more rapid and powerful the change will be. If you are patient, persevering, and persistent, your personal affirmation will take on a life of its own and change your inner reality according to the words you have spoken.

Make positive affirmations a regular part of your life. Post written reminders of your worth, your abilities, and the abundance of the universe on walls and mirrors, on your refrigerator, in your car. As you recite these statements to yourself, they will become manifest in your life.

Sometimes we may desire something when, in fact, our Higher Self has something better planned for us. For this reason, conclude your affirmation by saying, "For the highest good of all concerned." This way, you will know that your will and the will of your Higher Self are in harmony. When you have programmed your subconscious mind with only positive thoughts, you will be closer to achieving your goal of enlightenment.

We not only need to program the subconscious mind; it is also important to be able to retrieve information when it is needed. The part of a computer where information can be inserted and extracted when needed is referred to as the "memory." Our own memory is also involved in the process of recalling what we have learned and retained. Some people have excellent memories, while others have poor memories. Memory tends to improve up to the time of maturity. After that, there may be a very gradual decline in the ability to remember things. Time by itself, however, does not produce loss of memory. Research indicates that mental faculties don't have to decline as we grow older. If we remain physically and mentally healthy and active, our brains are also capable of staying healthy.

An emotional shock or an accident sometimes causes a person to experience amnesia where he can't retrieve the memories that were stored in his subconscious mind. He has forgotten, at least in his conscious mind, things that happened before the amnesia occurred, but he will probably be able to remember what has happened afterward.

Recording information in the subconscious mind cannot take place without the involvement of the conscious mind. If we are stressed, depressed, or tired, we may not be focusing on what is going on around us; therefore, the conscious mind does not send data to be stored in the memory. Sometimes what we hear "goes in one ear and out the other." We didn't concentrate on what was being said. The same is true of what we see. Whether or not we pay attention and concentrate on what we are observing will determine what we remember. All of us tend to filter out what isn't relevant to us. If we didn't, we would be overwhelmed with information. It's just that sometimes we make mistakes and filter out the information that really was relevant.

The way we first take in information and store it in the subconscious mind determines how well we will be able to access that information at a later time. Rather than just memorizing information that has little or no meaning, we need to understand the meaning of what we are learning and connect this new knowledge with things that we have previously learned. Knowledge that we are genuinely interested in is usually easy to remember.

Forgetfulness has to do with not being able to recall names, places, or things. Occasionally we may find ourselves in situations where we can't remember the name of a person that we know very well. Or maybe there is something that is right on the tip of the tongue, but we just can't quite remember it. Later, when we stop trying to remember, the answer may pop into our mind. Forgetting certain things doesn't mean we have a serious problem, but anxiety about it can create its own problems. Our attitude can be a major factor in our ability to recall information. Instead of believing that we have a poor memory, we can be optimistic about our mental abilities. We can help our memory by writing things down or repeating information like a name or directions. If there is an item, such as keys or glasses, that we are always misplacing, we need to have a specific place where we always put them. My mother used to say to me, "Have a place for everything and put everything in its place." This is still good advice.

When we review and use the information and knowledge that is stored in our memory and keep it active, we are less likely to forget it. Jean and I were best friends all through high school. Even after we graduated, married, and moved away, Jean and I still got together a couple of times a year. Jean loved to reminisce. She remembered many things that I had completely forgotten. She could remember the teachers we had, where we had gone on our double dates, and who came to our school dances. Jean would go over and over these past events each time we got together, keeping her memories alive.

Sometimes an experience may be so frightening that it is filed away in the depths of the subconscious mind and forgotten. Even after all the years that I have been a counselor, I am still shocked at the long-term trauma and devastation in people's lives caused by child abuse, rape, and incest. No one knows why some children remember and others forget an extremely painful experience such as rape or incest. How could anyone have forgotten such a life-changing event? Repression begins with blocking out the experience and pushing it into a hidden corner of the mind. No one is certain how often repression happens.

Some people may never remember the abuse. Others begin to remember their trauma when their Higher Self feels that they no longer need to repress the terror of their past. Sometimes the memories flood back spontaneously. At other times a television show or a story in a magazine will trigger the memory. Sometimes the memory returns when the person's own child reaches the age that she was when the trauma began. The entire event is stored in the subconscious mind; however, it may not be accurately recalled, because the memory may have been influenced by family stories, movies, or books. Memory before the age of three is not reliable because of the child's inability to interpret the experience.

Researchers have discovered that the subconscious mind is incapable of telling the difference between reality and fantasy, between a real experience and an imagined experience. This is why some people have had false memories; that is, they remember something that never really happened. They may be tuning into something they saw at the movies or on television. Perhaps they read it in a book or magazine. It is even possible that they were tuning into an experience that happened in a past life. To these people, their false memories are as vivid as the real experience. They may believe that they were sexually abused or raped when, in fact, the experience was only in their imagination.

Sometimes therapy is necessary to help sort out truth from fantasy. When looking for a therapist, try to find one who keeps an open mind and will not bring her personal beliefs into the therapy session. There are some therapists who wrongly believe that all eating disorders, loss of interest in sex, depression, or low self-esteem are linked to childhood sex abuse.

Once the regressed memories have been brought into the conscious mind, they need to be dealt with and finally resolved. Some therapists suggest that the person confront the abuser. But I have found that in most cases there is only denial by everyone who was involved, resulting in even more confusion. It is important to understand that despite what happened, most of the abusers did the best they knew under the circumstances. All too often, they were also abused as children. To be able to forgive an abuser who caused so much pain and anguish, we need to ask the Higher Self for help. With his help, it is possible to let go of the feeling of being a victim, and thus become a victor.

Susan is one of those who has become a victor. Life for her had been one failure and defeat after another. Susan grew up in an atmosphere of abuse. Both her father and her older brother sexually abused her from the time she was six years old. Her mother was too weak and frightened to intervene. Susan was beaten and put into a closet for long periods of time if she didn't cooperate with her father's sexual brutality. To escape this environment, Susan married in her teens. However, her husband continued the physical abuse. Often he would knock Susan down on the floor and then kick and stomp on her. By the time Susan was twenty-five, she had experienced so many broken bones that she had lost count. During this time, Susan gave birth to three children, two boys and a girl. One day when Susan came home from shopping, she found her husband sexually abusing her daughter. That was the day Susan made up her mind to escape. With the help and encouragement of a friend, Susan left her husband, got a divorce, and entered college. When she graduated with a degree in psychology, Susan was recognized for her achievement in turning her life around. In a ceremony honoring her in Washington, D.C.,

Susan received a Life Achievement Award. She now works at a shelter for abused women. It has been a long, difficult path, but Susan is no longer a victim; she is a victor.

The medical and scientific professions often use the term "unconscious" to mean the same as "subconscious." It is my opinion that these are separate parts of our consciousness and that they have different functions. When I was young, I used to faint at the sight of blood. As time went by, I gradually overcame most of my fear, but I still remember the blackness of being unconscious. While I lay there unconscious, my heart was still beating, my stomach was still digesting food. In this context, I am using the term "unconscious mind" as it relates to the autonomic nervous system.

The brain receives a steady stream of signals from the body organs that enable it to control our life processes. It regulates the activity of many organs, including the stomach, bladder, heart, blood vessels, adrenal glands, and sweat glands. This control is largely automatic — hence the name. The autonomic nervous system has two main parts: the sympathetic and the parasympathetic. Many organs have nerves coming from both systems. Such nerves produce opposite reactions. For example, a nerve from one system speeds up the heartbeat, while a nerve from the other system slows it down.

Emotions affect the operation of our autonomic nervous system. Our nervous system doesn't know the difference between our emotions and reality. So if we are disturbed by certain negative emotions, the body responds as if something is threatening us physically. It is possible for us to change or modify our negative emotions through biofeedback. In that way, we can develop some degree of voluntary control over the unconscious mind. For example, we can train the mind to replace fear with faith or to replace anger with love. As the nervous system processes this new information, it will send a positive message to all of the body's cells.

Our brain is more complicated and more wonderful than any computer ever built. Our conscious mind receives messages from our eyes, ears, nose, and skin that tell us what is going on in the world around us. The subconscious mind takes this information and stores it as memories. The unconscious mind receives a steady stream of signals from our body organs that enables it to control life processes. Our brain selects and combines messages from the senses with our memories and emotions to form our various thoughts and reactions. This is what makes it possible for us to learn, think, and remember. It is what makes us who we are today.

6

Communicating through the Superconscious Mind

Physical	Conscious
Energy	Unconscious
Emotional	Subconscious
	Superconscious

Our superconscious mind is the connecting link between our physical self and our Higher Self. It connects us to the memories that are stored with our Higher Self, which include all of the knowledge gathered over eons of time and from untold past lives. Our superconscious mind puts us in touch with the wise, powerful, and ever-present mind of our Higher Self, which is the source of our highest thoughts, ideas, and dreams. When we have opened the direct line of communication with our Higher Self, we will be able to tap into all this power and wisdom and it will become a potent, active part of our life.

Our conscious mind is aware of time, while our superconscious mind is aware of timelessness. Our Higher Self dwells in timelessness where there is no past or future, *only the eternal now*. It is my belief that the physical mind cannot fully comprehend the concept of the eternal now. Here in the physical world we experience linear time. We can remember the past. We are living in the present. We can only dream about the future, because the physical brain cannot record what it has not yet experienced.

We enter a physical body to learn certain lessons, to gain wisdom, and to learn how to express love. In a physical time dimension, this can only be accomplished by moving forward. As we move forward through time, the physical body deteriorates and eventually dies. Our brain also dies, but all that is stored in our memory has been transmitted through our superconscious mind to our Higher Self. All the experiences and knowledge of this lifetime, along with those of all our other lifetimes, are stored with our Higher Self who is ageless and timeless.

From the moment of birth until death, all that happens to us is being recorded. In modern terms, we can say that our lives are being video-recorded. All of these past-life videotapes are stored with our Higher Self. Because our Higher Self experiences timelessness, these tapes are equally accessible, regardless of when the past life was lived. It is just as easy for us to view a life lived in ancient Atlantis as it is to be regressed to a life lived in the 1800s.

One of the ways our Higher Self communicates with us is through our intuition. When an inner source of knowledge comes spontaneously through our superconscious mind, we call it a "hunch" or "intuition." An intuitive thought usually slips into our conscious mind when we are in a relaxed state and often when we least expect it. Because the Higher Self is capable of sensing circumstances and events that could or will happen in the future, it is important that we learn how to recognize the signals that warn us of danger. Sometimes we may experience an overwhelming feeling of fear. At other times, when the circumstances are less urgent, we may experience the sensations of apprehension, suspicion, or hesitation. Even though we may not be consciously aware of the impending danger, we should not ignore our strong feelings or hunches. Following our intuition could save our life.

Sometimes it may be difficult to distinguish between a message from the superconscious and a thought from the conscious mind. If it is a real hunch, it will prove itself in the due course of time. Because it deals with things that are beyond the physical in time and space, no one but the person receiving the hunch is really able to judge or take action regarding it.

Another way our superconscious mind connects us with our Higher Self is through our dreams. Throughout the ages, dreams have mystified, warned, and guided people. Ancient records contain accounts of angels who made visitations and gave messages to people as they slept. Everyone dreams, but many people do not recall their dreams. Some remember only fragmented parts of a dream they had just before awakening and nothing about earlier dreams.

Experiencing a dream is like watching a story on television. Some dreams are pleasant, others are perplexing, while still others are frightening. Many dreams are related to events of the previous day. I have called these "junk dreams" because they are of little or no value to us. They are motivated by physical, mental, or emotional stress or even an external experience. Feeling chilled or hearing a loud noise, for example, may become a part of the dream.

Dreams coming from our Higher Self can give us

help in solving a problem, warn against a plan of action, or teach us spiritual wisdom. Although only a small part of the message may filter through to our conscious mind, the complete message is transferred to our subconscious where it is retained as a memory. Later we may read or hear something that "rings a bell," and the information that has been stored in our memory comes into our conscious mind. We may wonder where the thoughts came from, but we will feel comfortable with the information because we recognize it as Truth.

Meditation is probably the easiest and most direct way for us to get in touch with our Higher Self. Meditation quiets our mind so we can listen to the message being relayed through our superconscious mind from our Higher Self. The communication we receive is more like a feeling or knowing rather than an audible voice. So we need to listen with our heart rather than our ears to the message from our Higher Self.

We all need to discover our own unique way of meditating. Some people enjoy meditating in a group, while others prefer to be alone. For some five minutes is long enough, while others spend at least half an hour in meditation. Some people sit cross-legged on the floor, while others are more comfortable sitting on a chair or even lying down. Some enjoy soft, soothing music playing in the background. Others repeat a word or sacred phrase, such as *peace* or *om*. We are free to choose whatever way makes us feel the most receptive.

To meditate, we all need to relax, close our eyes, and become quiet. Any time we receive or send communications through the superconscious mind, we need to be in an altered state of consciousness, the alpha state. Scientists have discovered that although the right and left hemispheres of our brain work together, they have different functions. The left brain is the rational, logical hemisphere, while the right brain is creative and intuitive. When we enter the alpha state, we are turning off the left hemisphere and tuning into the intuitive right part of our brain.

In my classes on meditation, I remind my students, "When meditating, it is important that you provide yourself with a quiet environment. Turn off the telephone, put out the cat or dog, and ask not to be disturbed. You will need to find a quiet place where there will be as few distractions and as little noise from the outside world as is possible."

When all my students are sitting in comfortable chairs with their feet flat on the floor and their hands resting on their laps, I say to them, "Close your eyes and take a few slow, deep breaths. Let each part of your body relax into a restful feeling. You are in a state of quiet listening. Feel the love of your Higher Self around you. Now visualize a stream of White Light coming from your Higher Self and entering your crown center. Feel this light flowing through all your bodies, bringing peace and relaxation to every part of you. Be still. Nothing moves but your breath. Now bring into your mind a question that you need answered or a problem that needs clarification. Now listen for some clue as to how best to solve your problem, or for some words of wisdom and comfort that will help ease the situation. Listen with your heart to your superconscious mind as it relays the message from your Higher Self."

As the class members sit silently in an altered state of consciousness, some students write down the messages that they are receiving. They may receive words of comfort, such as "Be at peace" or "Let it go." Some may receive definite instructions on how to handle a difficult situation. Others simply experience a sense of comfort or ease concerning the situation. Often emotions well up from the depths of the Soul and tears come to their eyes as they feel the love of their Higher Self surrounding them.

It's important that we let go of our logical mind's previous analysis of the problem so that we are open to the information being received. Perhaps we are told that we need to let go of any resentment, hatred, guilt, or fear that surrounds the situation. Perhaps we need to confront the person who seems to be a part of the problem. Once we have received guidance from our Higher Self, it is up to us whether or not we follow through on the advice. Remember that our Higher Self gives suggestions but never makes decisions or choices for us.

When we are perplexed, confused, or wondering what decision to make, our Higher Self is always available to help us make the right choice. However, we may not always receive the answer to our questions while we are meditating. After we have asked for guidance, we need to be mentally responsive to our Higher Self's reply. The answer may come as an inner feeling or a hunch leading us to the right place at the right time. Perhaps we are directed to a bookstore where we are led to a book which answers our questions; or we may overhear a conversation or a lecture which provides the solution to our problem. The answer may come when our conscious mind is relaxed, or in the form of a dream while we are asleep. It is important that we are open and alert so that we will recognize the answer when it does come.

If you wish to begin meditating on your own, my suggestion is that before you begin, you write down a question you want answered. The question should be written in such a way that the answer will need to be more involved than a simple yes or no. Then enter an altered state of consciousness by closing your eyes and quieting yourself. Some people feel more comfortable keeping their eyes closed as they write; however, it is possible to remain in the alpha state even when you open your eyes. When a word comes into your mind, write it down. Often after the first few words are written down, the message will begin to flow. After you have completed your meditation and read what you have written, you may be greatly surprised at the beauty of the prose or poetry.

Meditation, while not particularly complex, does require commitment. Once we've developed the skill, we can experience the beneficial side effects of meditation: lower blood pressure, reduced levels of stress, and an increased sense of well-being.

Just as meditation is listening to our God Self, prayer is talking to our God Self. True prayers are really conversations with our Higher Self. There is nothing we cannot share with him. We can trust him completely with our most private thoughts and feelings. Prayer can be a positive, renewing force in our lives, bringing us closer to the divine love of God as it is channeled through our Higher Self.

Some people feel that prayers are only a way of asking for something that they want. Others think that prayer is useful only in times of emergency when all else has failed. This reminds me of a story I heard several weeks ago:

It had been stormy for several days. Mr. Wright watched as the rain fell in torrents and the river began to overflow its banks. Soon the streets were filled from curb to curb with swirling, muddy water. In a short while, the water started flooding houses in the low-lying area. When the water began flowing into his house, Mr. Wright became really worried. Finally, he realized that in order to survive, he would have to get up on his roof. Still the floodwaters rose. Mr. Wright, being a very religious man, began to pray to God, "Please, dear Lord, save me." He said it over and over again.

In about an hour, some men came by in a motorboat and yelled, "Climb down and we will take you to higher ground."

"No, thank you," Mr. Wright replied. "I have faith that God will rescue me." The water rose even higher as Mr. Wright continued to pray to God, "Please, Lord, save me from the floodwaters." As Mr. Wright was praying, he looked up and saw a helicopter hovering over his rooftop.

The pilot yelled down, "Do you need help?"

"No," replied Mr. Wright. "God is going to save me." For several more hours, the man clung to his rooftop. Finally his strength was gone and he slipped beneath the raging torrent.

When Mr. Wright walked through the gates of Heaven, St. Peter could tell that he was really angry. "What is wrong?" St. Peter asked.

Mr. Wright replied, "I prayed to God to rescue me and he let me drown."

Then a voice from above said, "I sent a boat and a helicopter to save you. What more could I do?"

The moral of the story is that God does answer emergency 911 calls, but he does it in His own way and in His own time.

Prayers differ according to the various religious beliefs. In ancient Egyptian and Greek temples and later in some early Christian churches, prayer wheels were hung in the place of worship and turned by the worshippers.

Turning the wheel was supposed to have the effect of repeating their prayers. Today in some Tibetan Buddhist temples they still use prayer wheels which have sacred writings or a prayer inscribed on them.

Prayer beads are of ancient origin and were probably first used by Buddhists. Both Buddhists and Muslims make use of them in their prayers. St. Dominic is said to have introduced their use into the Roman Catholic Church. The rosary is a string of beads on which prayers are counted as an aid to memory.

Some people kneel while they pray. Others sit, stand, or lie on the ground. Roman Catholics may pray to saints or to the Virgin Mary as well as to God. Others pray directly to the God Essence, their Higher Self. Some pray aloud, while others pray silently. No matter how we choose to pray, our earnest, heartfelt prayers are received with love.

Long, eloquent prayers aren't necessary. In fact, the words we use aren't that important either. It is the feeling behind the words that makes the difference. It doesn't do much good to repeat a lot of words that we aren't even thinking about. The constant repetition of words, no matter how beautiful the prose, will not be as effective as simple words that come from our heart. We can converse with our Higher Self with a feeling of intimacy, as we would talk with a close friend, because our Higher Self is our closest and best friend.

It really doesn't matter where we choose to pray. Some people may prefer to pray in a church or synagogue. Others feel more comfortable in the privacy of their own homes. Still others may feel closer to God while they are enjoying nature, perhaps at the beach or in the woods. Personally, I feel comfortable talking to my Higher Self wherever I am. Sometimes I travel astrally to a higher plane where I have created, with my mind, a beautiful, little chapel with stained-glass windows. This is a very holy, personal place where my Higher Self and I can share time together.

All sincere prayers are answered; however, they may not be answered in the way we were expecting. Our Higher Self knows what is best for us, so sometimes the answer may be "no." At other times, the answer may be "not yet," because the timing is not right. When we end our prayers by saying, "Thy will be done," we can relax and know that we will receive the right answer to our prayers.

I have a bumper sticker on my car that says "EXPECT A MIRACLE." By the standard definition, a miracle is an extraordinary, supernatural event that defies the natural laws of probability. However, to the Higher Self, the natural laws and the supernatural laws are the same. Our superconscious mind connects us to the miraculous healing power of our Higher Self. We can pray that our body and mind be healed from all disease. When we pray for a miraculous healing, we need to open our mind and heart and expect a miracle. With an attitude of faith and expectancy, we can create our own miracles.

With the help of our Higher Self, it is possible for us to send healing energies to someone else through our prayers. Because these energies are spiritual, it doesn't matter how far away we are from the person needing our prayers. The power of our prayer is determined by our sincere emotions, not by the words we use. Our prayers for a person's healing are directed through the ethers until they reach their target. Psychically, prayers appear as shining white wings of love that tenderly enfold the one to whom they are sent. Our prayers are effective in healing because they bring new energies to the person. When we pray for healing, we also need to pray that God's will be done. Then we can ignore any of our doubts and expect a miracle.

Our prayers are not only able to bring healing energies to others; they can also provide a person with a shield of protection. How effective we are is determined by the intensity and concentration of our thoughts. We need to picture the person as vividly as possible and then clearly present the ideas we wish to convey. As we are praying for someone's protection, with the help of our Higher Self, our thoughts will form a shield of white light around that person. This shield will remain for a time proportionate to the strength of our thoughts. It will guard against negative or hostile thoughts and can even ward off physical dangers. If we send someone thoughts of peace, it will soothe and quiet the mind, encircling the person with an atmosphere of calm. What a wonderful gift we can give to our family members and friends when we take the time to pray earnestly for their protection and peace of mind!

Without taking away the free will of a person, we can make a difference in someone's life. Again, we need to picture the person as vividly as possible. Then with our full attention, we can impress our thoughts upon the person's mind. Success depends on the concentration and the steadiness of our thoughts. This is especially powerful when the person is asleep and thus more open to receiving our thoughts telepathically. Our efforts should be directed toward placing positive thoughts and ideas into the person's mind. This can give someone the incentive to let go of a negative habit, or help them make the right choice in a difficult situation. However, our thoughts cannot make people do something that they don't want to do. It does not take away their free will.

Through our superconscious mind, we can communicate with our Higher Self. Communication means an exchange of information. The goal of communicating with our Higher Self is to be able to understand as well as to be understood. To be able to understand, we need to perfect the art of listening. We need to listen intuitively to the thoughts, ideas, and feelings of our Higher Self. To be understood, we need to clearly express our desires, needs, and concerns through prayer. Prayer has the power to lift us up out of poverty, depression, or sickness. It can heal the sick and accomplish the seemingly impossible. We need to have faith in our indwelling God and know that our Higher Self is guiding and directing us toward success, happiness, health, and peace of mind. One of our supreme attainments in the physical world is to become conscious of and in communication with our beloved Higher Self through meditation, dreams, intuition, and prayer.

7

Educating the Soul

The whole purpose of coming into the physical world is to educate our Soul. Earth is very much like a giant classroom. Before we incarnated, we chose certain lessons to learn and tests to pass. Some of us have enjoyed the challenge: we have studied hard, done our homework, and received high grades. Others, however, appear to be either rebellious or lazy. They seem to have forgotten what classes they signed up for, and they appear to have no desire to succeed. Everyone has free will. No truant officer will haul us into the classroom or stand over us to see that we finish our homework. It is our choice whether we learn our lessons or whether we waste our time in extracurricular activities. Those who do not pass the tests will be given another opportunity to learn these lessons in another time and another place.

Although people have different interests, we all have the same major. That major is *love*. We are all attending Earth's school to learn this lesson. We will continue to study it until we finally comprehend the true meaning of love and are able to live a life of unconditional, nonjudgmental love.

We each have a personal counselor who is available to give us advice and encouragement. He knows the lessons we have chosen to learn. He also knows whether we have passed or failed these lessons. This personal counselor is our Higher Self, who is a very important part of our life. Without his guidance we would probably not be able to attain our Master's degree — the Master of Self and the Art of Love degree.

Our physical, energy, and emotional bodies are vehicles for the soul body. When we leave the physical world through death, we leave our physical and energy bodies behind where they decay and return to dust. When we leave the astral world through death, we leave behind our emotional body, where it, too, disintegrates. We are not the physical body. We are not the energy or emotional bodies. We are the Soul which dwells within the eternal soul body.

One of the great mysteries of life pertains to our Soul. Most religions teach that there is something in humans that survives bodily death and that a Soul is distinguishable from and superior to the physical body. They believe that the physical body is created as a dwelling place for the Soul. Some religions refer to the Soul as the abode of the Holy Spirit. In Oriental literature, the Soul and the Self are synonymous. Plato believed that though the body dies and disintegrates, the Soul continues to live forever.

Aristotle regarded the Soul as the true Being in the physical body.

Speculation as to where the Soul is to be found within the human body has been constant throughout human history. In the past, many great men, including Plato and Hippocrates, said that the Soul was in the brain. But there was disagreement as to what part of the brain — the forepart, cerebellum, medulla, fourth ventricle, or pineal gland. Others said that the seat of the Soul was in the heart. Some said the Soul was not just in the brain but also extended to the spinal cord, nerves, arteries, veins, internal organs, and nervous system. Finally, it was realized that the Soul is not found in just one part of our body but that it encompasses our total being. Our soul body, containing the God essence, interpenetrates every cell of our emotional, energy, and physical bodies. We cannot be separated from our soul body because it is our real self. When we have laid down our other bodies through death, we will be dwelling in our eternal soul body.

Another question that has continued to be debated has to do with the composition of the Soul. The Egyptians believed that the Soul was formed of a divine ray acting through a fluid-like substance. Hindus teach that the human Soul is a portion of an immutable principle called the Soul of the World. Aristotle regarded the Soul as the sum of the vital principles. Plato believed that the Soul has three parts and that the immortal part comes from God. According to Eastern beliefs, the Soul contains *prana*, the life principle. Prana unites spirit and matter and helps the Soul carry out its divine purpose. Christian mystics believe that there dwells in each Soul a potential which they call "Christ in you" that enables every person to eventually attain the status of Master or Christ. Many Christians believe that the Soul is the dwelling place of the Holy

Spirit. There are others who believe that the Soul contains the essence of God, the divine spirit. Regardless of the words used, all agree that the Soul is composed of an energy that originates with God.

Our Soul receives its life-force from our Higher Self, and our Higher Self receives its life-force from God. To understand this abstract concept, let us consider how electricity reaches our home. Large generators in power stations produce electrical power, which is sent over transmission lines. This voltage is too high for local users, so when the electric power reaches the area where it will be used, transformers lower the voltage. But our home needs still lower voltage, which is obtained through transformers fastened to the poles that support the wires running to houses. Because the energy that flows from God Almighty is so powerful, we need to have it transformed by our Higher Self into energy that our Soul is capable of using. Just as the electrical current that comes into our homes can be turned on or off by switches, we are also able to turn on or off the flow of the Essence of God. As we strive for enlightenment, we will learn how to keep the power turned on all the time.

Whenever we ask for the White Light of protection or healing, we turn on the flow of God's energy. The White Light of healing enters through our crown center at the top of our head and flows through every one of our bodies, bringing emotional as well as physical healing. When we ask for the White Light to protect us, it also enters at the top of our head and flows to our soul body, where it provides additional strength and protection for our other bodies.

Our soul body not only interpenetrates the cells of our other bodies but extends past them. For those who are not very spiritual, the soul body extends only a few inches past the emotional body and appears to be opaque. As we become more spiritual, the soul body becomes larger and begins to glow with an inner radiance. When we approach enlightenment, our Soul becomes gloriously iridescent and opalescent. The Soul of a Master often extends several feet past the physical body and shines with an inner luminescent splendor.

Because our soul body extends past our physical body, we may feel uncomfortable if we sit so close to someone that our soul bodies overlap. If the person we are sitting beside is a stranger who has negative vibrations, after a short time we may become edgy and upset as we pick up that person's negativity. If the person is of like vibrations or is someone we love, the feeling we may experience is one of joy and contentment.

Our Soul contains within itself the essence of all that is positive and good in each of our lives. All the good that is stored within the Soul can never be lost. While negativity and evil cannot be stored in the Soul, they can affect the soul body and can dim its luminosity.

The real purpose of life on Earth is to educate the Soul. This can be a long and sometimes difficult experience. Every physical life is an opportunity for Soul growth and the development of spiritual powers. The education of our Soul is very personal and unique. Our Soul records the state of evolution that we have attained. The Souls of each one of us are learning at a different pace. No one learns at the same rate, nor are we learning the same lessons. Because we have free will, we do not have to evolve. Through inaction or ignorance, we can choose not to learn the lessons of life.

It is not for us to judge how far someone else has evolved. Perhaps someone is spiritually evolved but still has much to learn regarding relationships with others. One person may be very immature in matters concerning patience or forgiveness, while another may already have learned these lessons. It is important that we do not try to compare our progress with anyone else's.

Educating the Soul is more difficult for some people than for others. When we have finally learned a specific lesson, it is recorded on our *spiritual transcript* and we do not need to learn that lesson again. Let us say that Dick is just finishing the fifth grade. He really hasn't tried very hard in class. He hasn't done any homework or learned the lessons the teacher gave him, so when he takes the final test, he fails. No matter how poorly Dick has done in fifth grade, though, he won't be sent back to the third or fourth grade; he has already passed the tests for those grades. The principal calls Dick into the office and explains that he will have to take the fifth grade over again. The problem is that Earth will no longer have the elementary grades, so Dick will have to transfer to another planet to continue the education of his Soul.

Let us say that Jane has just finished the tenth grade. She has studied hard and done quite well with her lessons. She passed all her finals with flying colors — except for patience. She is really disappointed that she has failed this lesson. The principal calls Jane into the office and explains she will have to repeat patience next semester, but she will receive special help so she can pass her finals next time.

It is the quality of our Soul that really gives life meaning. We live in two worlds-the outer, physical world, and an inner, spiritual one. We must understand both before we can make sense of our life down here on Earth. It is our inner world that determines our outer life, and not the other way around. Our Soul is a part of the inner world and is influenced by the superconscious mind, which draws its wisdom and guidance from the Higher Self. Our physical selves are a part of the outer world and are influenced by the subconscious mind and our past programming, which is sometimes based on illusion or fear. As we approach enlightenment, we will experience a shift from a material to a spiritual, purposeful life.

Without the soul body, our Higher Self would have no vehicle for expression in the physical world. Our physical, energy, and emotional bodies are transient; they wear out and are replaced, time after time. Our eternal Soul is the pure essence of God which has taken on a form in order to experience a life in time and space. The purpose of our physical life is to make it possible for our Soul to learn the lessons of life and love.

The highest vibration, the most powerful energy is love. The key to transforming our soul body into its true magnificence is love. This love is more than passionate love, more than brotherly love: it is spiritual love. Spiritual love is unconditional and nonjudgmental. The greatest miracle of all occurs when we advance into our own spiritual perfection and become enlightened. Then our soul body will be transformed into an opalescent body of light and love.

In the Celestial World, our soul body is as visible and substantial as our physical body is here on Earth. When we enter into the higher realms, we will let go of our finite bodies and we will once again dwell in our eternal soul body.

8

In the Beginning

<u>Almighty—Prime Creator</u>
|
<u>Universal Lords</u>
|
<u>Solar Lords</u>
|
<u>Planetary Lords</u>
|
Humanity

The creation of Earth and the people who call this planet home is one of the most fascinating stories of all time. All early races had their own creation myths which they considered sacred and completely true. These ancient myths tried to explain the origin of the world and the creation of humanity. Most myths included divine beings who had supernatural powers, yet the gods and goddesses of mythology had human characteristics, too. In most cases, these gods and goddesses were patterned after the highly evolved beings whom we would identify as angelic or extraterrestrial.

Both the Christian Bible and the Torah, the Jewish scriptures, include the book of Genesis. The word "genesis" means "origin" or "coming into being" and is the story of creation. The theme of human origin, as written in Genesis, has much in common with the literature of

Babylon, Canaan, and Egypt, and with myths in many other lands around the world. Hesiod, one of the great poets of ancient Greece, wrote that the universe began in a state of emptiness called "Chaos." The goddess Gaea (Earth) arose out of Chaos. She immediately gave birth to Uranus, who became king of the sky. Gaea mated with Uranus, producing children called the Titans.

All over the world, similar stories of the creation of Earth were related by ancient people who were unaware of one another's existence. One such creation myth comes from a little island in the Pacific Ocean about four hundred fifty miles northeast of Tahiti. "In the beginning there was only empty space, neither darkness nor light, neither land nor sea, neither sun nor sky. Everything was a big, silent void. Untold ages went by. Then the void began to move. New strange forces were at work. The night was transformed. The sand became firm ground that grew upwards. Lastly, Earth Mother revealed herself and spread abroad and became a great country. There were plants, animals, and fish in the water and they multiplied. The only thing that was lacking was man. Then Tangaloa created Tiki, who was our first ancestor."

There is no single, generally accepted scientific theory as to how the Earth and our solar system were formed. Some scientists believe that the solar system may have developed from a huge cloud of gas and dust that once swirled around the Sun. The Sun itself may have been formed from the central part of this nebula. As the nebula whirled around the Sun, it slowly flattened out. Sections of the cloud began to spin like whirlpools. Gas and dust collected near the centers of these eddies. The collections of gas and dust grew by attracting nearby particles of matter. These may have slowly developed into the spinning planets that now travel around the Sun.

Other scientists propose the double star theory. Our galaxy contains many two-star combinations called double stars. Perhaps the Sun and a companion star were once double stars. The companion star may have exploded into a cloud of gas and debris which was captured by the Sun's gravity. The planets could have developed from this exploded star.

It never ceases to amaze me how insignificant Earth is in relationship to the universe. It is but a small part of our solar system centered around the Sun, which is only an average-sized star. Our solar system itself is not especially impressive, in spite of the fact that it is about ten billion miles in diameter. It belongs to the Milky Way galaxy, a vast complex of stars. Even the Milky Way is not that impressive when compared with the total number of galaxies in the universe. There may be millions of galaxies, each with billions of stars, and many of the stars may have systems that include habitable planets. Some astronomers estimate that the universe may teem with more than one hundred billion habitable worlds. We've come a long way since the time when it was believed that Earth was the center of the universe and the only place where life could exist.

Although we actually know little for certain about the nature of creation, there are several theories concerning the origin of the universe. Some maintain that the universe came into being by accident. Then, through a gradual process of chance and evolution, it progressed from a simple state to its present complexity. But this theory does not explain how the original matter came into being.

Another belief is the traditional religious viewpoint that God is the creator of the universe. This belief and the Big Bang theory of modern science are slowly moving closer together. The Big Bang theory states that billions of years ago, all matter in the universe was compressed into a single, original atom. Then, with incredible force, this mass exploded. One second after the explosion, some of the conditions that make life possible were already established. Two forces capable of acting over large distances are gravity and electromagnetic force, which is much stronger than gravity. This electromagnetic force is canceled out because positive protons and negative electrons have equal charges. When the universe was about a second old, if either the protons or electrons had had a slightly higher charge than the other, the electromagnetic force would have overwhelmed gravity. Without the effect of gravity, there would be no galaxies, no stars, no planets, and no life as we know it.

Many believe that the original force, God, who knew what the results would be, caused all the worlds in the universe to originate from this tremendous explosion of the primordial atom. Thus, the galaxies with their billions and billions of stars came into being. These galaxies are still expanding from the force of the explosion. If the matter composing all the stars came from the same original mass, it is only logical that the stars and planets in all the galaxies are made of the same elements and function within the same laws.

The philosopher Philo, who lived during the time of Jesus, taught that there were many powers or spirits that radiate from God. He also said that everything in the universe is an expression or idea in the mind of God. Just as a beautiful thought is created or an idea is born, everything that came into being was an aspect of the mind of the Prime Creator, God. Thus, the Spirit of God moved over the face of the universe, and out of chaos came order and beauty.

Cosmic wisdom states that the primary motive behind the creation of the universe was to have a dwelling place for the companions of God Almighty. The first created beings were androgynous and perfect. They are the great Archangels or Universal and Cosmic Lords. These Great Beings are attuned to the supreme will of God and are the companions of the Prime Creator, as they were intended to be. Since they possess free will, each manifests in a slightly different way from all the others.

The Archangels began to experiment with the power of their own creative individuality. Using the blueprint of God Almighty, they created other perfect androgynous beings who became the Solar Lords. These Solar Lords were given the responsibility of governing the various solar systems. Later, the Solar Lords took it on themselves to create other beings, the Planetary Lords. These Planetary Lords, in turn, are responsible for caring for the individual planets in each solar system.

Now it came to pass that a call was sent out to Planetary Lords asking for volunteers to come and take part in helping prepare a new planet, Terra (Earth), for human life. Each group of Lords was assigned a specific section of the Earth as their responsibility. The first thing they did was to seed the land with a variety of grasses, plants, bushes, and trees, which each Lord brought from their home planet.

After a long time had passed, these Planetary Lords returned to Terra. They were pleased to see that Earth had become a garden covered with trees and plants. This time they brought with them many different kinds of fish, reptiles, mammals, and birds from their home planets. With their advanced knowledge of DNA, they were also able to create new species. Some of these animals could not adjust to their new environment and perished. Others not only survived but thrived and multiplied.

Because the Planetary Lords had been assigned to different parts of Earth, each section had its own unique varieties of animals and plants. When the plants and animals were flourishing, the Planetary Lords knew it was time to create humans. There are many theories but no firm scientific facts that tell how the different races came into being, except that they have existed since the earliest times. Many myths and traditions of ancient religions say that the gods created humans in their own image. Myths also relate how certain gods guided their particular races, protecting them from hostile influences. Although the races differ from one another in certain characteristics, they all belong to a single biological species. If the Planetary Lords, whom we might identify as angelic beings or extraterrestrials, were masters of interstellar space travel and possessed superior technological knowledge, they were probably experts in genetic manipulation. They could use their knowledge of DNA to clone or create humans. So each Lord, using technically advanced knowledge of the life force and DNA, created mankind in his own image, with a particular color of hair, eyes, and skin, and particular body and facial traits. They then passed on to these humans a part of the God essence — a Soul.

According to cosmic wisdom, channeled through Edgar Cayce, there was not just one place that could be called the "cradle of mankind." There were at least five different places on Earth that were considered gardens of Eden because each group of Planetary Lords had been given a specific section of Earth as their responsibility. The white race was believed to have been located in Iran, the Caucasus along the Black Sea, and the Carpathian Mountains of central Europe. The yellow race probably settled in what was later to become the Gobi Desert of eastern Asia. The black race was believed to have been located in the Sudan and northwestern Africa. The brown race probably settled in the Andes and on Lemuria, a continent which in ancient times was located in the Pacific Ocean.

The red race was believed to have been located in America and on Atlantis, a continent which at that time was in the Atlantic Ocean.

According to the Bible, Adam and Eve were the parents of the human race. The word "Adam" comes from the Hebrew word meaning "man." Some consider Adam and Eve not as individuals who lived at a certain time and place, but far more relevant to us, as timeless archetypes of human nature: male and female, Adam and Eve, each possessing a dual nature. Others believe that Adam was an individual but that he was also the symbol of the whole race of Sons of God who chose to enter a physical body and become inhabitants of planet Earth.

When I was about ten years old, I asked my Sunday school teacher, "If Adam and Eve were the parents of all the people on Earth, how did Cain get his wife?" My teacher had just read to us the Bible story of Adam and Eve's sons, Cain and Abel. When Cain killed his brother Abel in a fit of rage, Cain was forced to leave his home. "So Cain went out from the presence of the Lord and settled in the land of Nod, east of Eden. Then Cain's wife conceived and she bore him a son named Enoch" (Gen. 4:16-17a). If all humans came from Adam and Eve, then how can we explain the fact that other humans were living at the same time in the land of Nod?

Cosmic tradition says that some of the Planetary Lords who were involved in the preparation of Earth and the creations of the Earthians felt a great love for their creation. So they approached the Solar Lords and asked for permission to take physical bodies so that they could live in the physical world. The mighty Archangels agreed to the request, with one exception. These Planetary Lords would no longer express as one being but as two separate beings. One would remain in the higher dimension, still perfect and androgynous, while the other would be allowed to enter a physical body and experience life on Earth. Some of the Planetary Lords agreed to this stipulation and went through a process to become two separate beings. Thus they became Twin Souls.

Some have confused the terms "soul mate" and "Twin Soul." A soul mate is someone we have been with in many lifetimes: as parent and child, as siblings, as husband and wife, or as close friends in both the physical and astral dimensions. Usually the bond of love becomes stronger and more intense with each incarnation. Sometimes our soul mate is the same sex as we are. In one lifetime we may not find a soul mate, while in another lifetime we may meet several soul mates.

We have only one Twin Soul who dwells in the higher dimensions. There are many names for our Twin Soul: Twin Flames, Higher Self, Guardian Angel, Holy Spirit, and God Self. It matters not what name we use as long as we remember that we are one with our Twin Soul who remains in the higher realm, still androgynous and still perfect.

Not all of the Planetary Lords had the same reason for desiring to take on a physical body in order to live on Terra. Some fell in love with the beautiful human women and desired to become sexually involved with them. Others chose to come into the physical world to become teachers and spiritual guides for the newly created Earthians. Regardless of their reasons for desiring to live on Terra, many of them began to collect karmic debts that needed to be paid. So they found themselves in a position where they had to incarnate again and again to repay their debts.

In the sixth chapter of Genesis it says, "Now a population explosion took place upon the Earth. It was at this time that beings from the spirit world (Sons of God) looked upon the beautiful Earth women and took any they desired to be their wives ... In those days, and even afterwards when the Sons of God were sexually involved with human women, their children became giants, of whom so many legends are told" (Gen. 6:1,2,4).

The Earthians worshiped many gods. Some of their gods are known to us as nature spirits, angels, Archangels, and extraterrestrials. Nearly all ancient civilizations worshiped the sun because they knew that nothing could survive without it. The Egyptians revered their sun god, Ra. The ancient Greeks had their own sun god, Helios, while the Romans worshiped Sol, which is Latin for "sun." The Inca rulers called themselves "sons of the Sun" and traced their origin to the sun god Inti. But along with their assortment of gods, these ancient civilizations also recognized a Supreme Being. The Hebrews were probably the first to introduce the concept of one God. The Christian religion (Protestant and Catholic) bases its beliefs on the Old Testament and continues the concept of one God, but as part of the Trinity — the unity of Father, Son, and Holy Spirit.

In the Bible there are eight Hebrew and nine Greek terms pertaining to God. Some believe that all these names refer to one great Being; others feel that they refer to different aspects of God. For example, the names Almighty God, Eternal God, and God of Gods pertain to the Prime Creator. The names Lord of Lords, Lord God, and Lord of Hosts refer to Universal and Solar Lords, while the names Jehovah and Heavenly Father refer to Planetary Lords.

The Planetary Lord Jehovah is considered to be the protector and spiritual leader of the Hebrews. He is concerned with their welfare as a nation. There is an interesting verse in Exodus that says, "And God spoke to Moses and said to him: 'I am the Lord. I appeared to Abraham, to

Isaac, and to Jacob, as God Almighty, but by my name, Jehovah (Jahweh), I was not known to them'" (Exodus 6:2-3, King James version). Does this verse mean that the Planetary Lord Jehovah had identified himself to Abraham and the others as God Almighty?

The great God of the universe, the Prime Creator, is not to be confused with the gods of ancient myths nor with the Universal, Solar, or Planetary Lords. The terms "omnipotent" (unlimited authority and influence), "omnipresent" (present in all places at all times), and "omniscient" (infinite awareness, understanding, and wisdom) have always been used to describe God Almighty. This emphasizes the fact that God is indeed Spirit. Each atom in the universe contains a spark of light, the spirit of God. God's Spirit dwells within every atom of every rock, plant, animal, and living being in the whole universe. God lives, works, loves, and creates through many Great Beings such as the Archangels and Lords, as well as through you and me!

The universe is governed by simple cosmic laws. The first is the Law of Love. Through love, God Almighty brought forth the first perfect Beings, the Universal and Cosmic Lords. The second law is one of propagation. The Prime Creator gave to these great Archangels the power and wisdom to continue the process of creation. They in turn, using God Almighty's blueprints, created other perfect beings. The third law is the Law of Evolution, or growth and development. Angels and humans alike have the opportunity to grow and evolve in wisdom and in love.

9

Tracing Our Ancestry

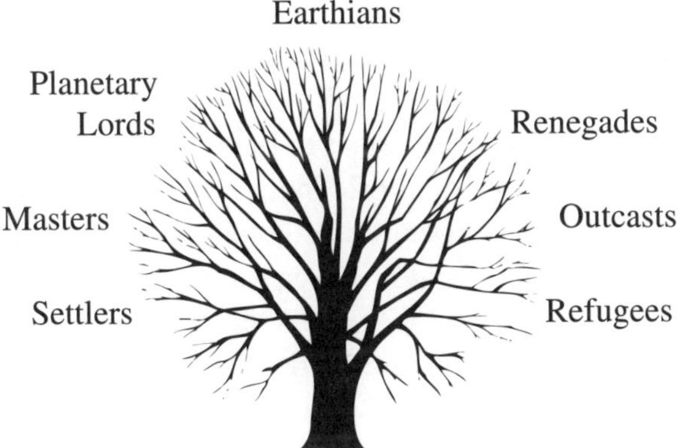

Tracing our ancestry can be an exciting experience. As in any genealogy, we may find some we are proud to call our ancestors, while we may be ashamed to discover that others are a part of our family tree.

The original inhabitants of Terra, the Earthians, were joined by some of the Planetary Lords who chose to take on physical bodies. Children were born of these unions. As time passed, refugees, outcasts, settlers, and spiritual teachers came to Earth from other planets in our solar system. Some even came from solar systems deep in the heart of the galaxy. Ancient Sumerian texts from 6000 B.C. tell in great detail of the coming of tall, shining gods who built cities and established highly advanced civilizations. This same basic story is retold in Assyrian, Babylonian, Egyptian, Roman, and Greek myths.

In Earth's history, many different extraterrestrial groups came to share their superior technology with Earthians. Many of the extraterrestrials who came to Terra mated with the Earthians. In time, as the inhabitants of Earth intermarried, there was a blending of the various races and the different kinds of people.

Some of those who joined the original inhabitants of Earth were outcasts who were sent to Earth from other planets in our solar system just as England once sent her outcasts to Australia. In 1778, eleven sailing vessels left England bound for Australia. On board were convicts, desperate criminals, political prisoners, petty lawbreakers, and poor people who had been imprisoned for debt. During the eighty years that Australia served as a penal colony, Great Britain sent about 168,000 prisoners there. It was not until 1868 that England discontinued this practice of shipping outcasts to Australia.

For eons, Earth has been the penal colony for our solar system. Cosmic tradition tells us that several planets, including Venus, sent their outcasts to Earth. These were inhabitants who were rebellious troublemakers. They were filled with negativity and so could no longer remain on their home planet. These renegades may be what the Bible and other ancient writings refer to as "fallen angels." When it was time for them to reincarnate, their Souls were placed in the fetuses of Earth mothers. Some of these outcasts have not yet learned the lesson of love. They are still causing problems here on Earth.

Great changes are happening to Mother Earth at this time. Soon Earth will be moving from the third to the fourth dimension. When this occurs, all the renegades and those who have not raised their vibrations through love will no longer be allowed to incarnate on this planet. They will be sent to another planet being prepared for them where they can continue learning the lessons of love.

Some of the inhabitants of Earth came here as refugees from another planet. According to ancient tradition, there was once a planet between Mars and Jupiter, which has been identified by the names Maldek and Lucifer. It is believed that Maldek's force field had been severely weakened by a long nuclear war. Many of the Higher Beings had abandoned the struggle and emigrated to other planets. Either as the result of a collision with a comet, or from the nuclear war, or by a combination of the two, Maldek was destroyed. Astronomers have tried to explain how and why this planet exploded. There is now a gap of three hundred million miles between Mars and Jupiter. This is not empty space, but a region containing thousands of rocks, known as the Asteroid Belt. This may be all that remains of Maldek. Because of the destruction of this planet, the gravitational balance in our solar system was temporarily thrown into confusion. This catastrophe affected all the planets in our solar system and may have been the cause of a polar shift on Earth.

Some people believe that a few the inhabitants of Maldek were warned of the impending danger. A Planetary Lord by the name of Jehovah gathered a group of his people and transported them in spaceships to Earth to escape the catastrophe. Some believe that these refugees were the beginning of the Hebrew people on planet Earth.

There is a passage in Genesis that may refer to this event: "Now the Lord had said to Abram: 'Get out of your country, from your kindred and from your father's house, to a land that I will show you. I will make you a great nation; I will bless those who bless you, and I will curse him who curses you; and in you all the families of the earth shall be blessed.' So Abram departed as the Lord had spoken to him" (Gen. 12:1-4a). In these verses, the word

"Lord" probably refers to Jehovah, the Planetary Lord of the Hebrew nation. Would God Almighty be partial to one particular group of people, while *cursing* another group? No! God Almighty is not only impartial but is the Spirit of pure love.

Besides the refugees and outcasts who came to Earth, settlers arrived from other planets to establish colonies. One of their goals was to teach the Earthians a better way of life. It is believed that Lemuria was founded by some of these space settlers. Very little is known about Lemuria except that it was situated in the Pacific Ocean. It may have been a part of the much older civilization of Mu. It is believed that the Lemurian colonizers came from another planet or solar system in spaceships. They brought with them great knowledge and Truth.

They may also have brought with them some of their favorite foods, including the banana. The banana has been known in the tropical regions of Earth for many thousands of years, yet it does not usually multiply by seeds. The main stem dies after bearing one bunch of fruit. New banana plants are started by replanting shoots produced by the roots of a mature banana plant. There is an ancient myth that tells of the wonderful *Kandali* (banana bush) which Manu, the great protector of mankind, brought to our planet from another star which was much further along the path of evolution than Earth.

This ancient race knew a great deal more about manipulating the forces of nature than we do. Those who settled in Lemuria were not only technically but also spiritually advanced, and they hoped that by coming to Earth they could bring a higher consciousness to the Earthians. The ancient myths are full of gods who came down from the sky. To the people of Earth, they were thought of as ambassadors of the Supreme Being.

The Lemurians established colonies in many parts of the world. Perhaps at one time the Polynesian islands were either part of the continent of Lemuria or one of its colonies. The original inhabitants of Polynesia appear to have had a common language source and the same gods as well as the same legends and myths.

A strange legacy can be found on Easter Island. Along the coast there are hundreds of ancient stone statues, some weighing as much as seventy tons. Some of these statues are finished, while others are only partly carved. Some are standing upright while others appear to have been knocked over. Archaeologists are baffled and so far have not been able to give a convincing reason why a small group of Polynesians took such pains to carve these statues. Nor has anyone been able to discover the highly advanced techniques that were used to free the stone blocks from the hard lava and bring them to their present site. One of the Polynesian myths that has been handed down through the ages is that the colossal statues which are found on the coast of Easter Island landed in their positions *from the air by themselves*. Another mystery is the fact that these statues, with their long straight noses, narrow lips, sunken eyes, and low foreheads, look nothing like the native Polynesians. Perhaps these statues were carved by descendants of the Lemurians as a tribute to their ancestors.

Perhaps as the result of a polar shift, the continent of Lemuria sank beneath the Pacific Ocean as other land masses rose up out of the ocean floor. One theory contends that the poles have shifted several times in Earth's history, causing cataclysms in past ages. When the Earth's outer crust slipped, the magnetic poles moved away from the axial poles, causing the Earth to wobble on its axis. The shifting of the crust resulted in earthquakes, tidal waves, volcanic upheaval, melting glaciers, and rising ocean levels. The combination of all of these cataclysms may have caused the destruction of Lemuria. After Lemuria sank, the cultures of her colonies began to degenerate.

Some believe that the aboriginal people of Australia, as well as Japan, are descended from the Lemurian race. There is a small tribe living on the Japanese island of Hokkaido who still claim that they are the direct descendants of gods who came from the stars. Tradition says that the Maori of New Zealand were not originally earthborn people. The South Sea Islanders also say that their ancestors came from heaven and arrived on Earth in an enormous gleaming egg.

Some believe that the Hawaiian Islands are all that remains of Lemuria today. Others believe that the Caroline Islands are the only remaining land masses that were once a part of the Lemurian continent. From an archaeological viewpoint, there is evidence that at one time a great city existed on and around the Caroline Islands. The ruins start on the land and then continue down under the water. Divers have gone down more than two hundred feet and have found the ruins of huge structures, walls, and countless stone pillars. The divers told of walking on the ocean floor on well-preserved roads overgrown with mussels and coral. Legend says that these ruins hold a vast treasure in pearls, silver, and even platinum. It has been estimated from the size of the ruins that at one time the city may have been large enough to support a population of several million.

During the early history of Lemuria, Atlantis was not yet inhabited. The people of Lemuria were far more spiritually advanced than the Atlantians, and they did not misuse their powers as did the people of Atlantis. It is believed that Atlantis was a continent which existed in what is now the Atlantic Ocean. It is also believed that records of Atlantis will be found near the pyramids in

Egypt as well as in the Himalayas. These hidden records will one day provide more information about the existence of Atlantis.

The mystery of Atlantis has tantalized minds since Plato first wrote about it. Some people wonder if Atlantis really existed, or if it was invented by ancient storytellers. Plato said that in ancient times a great empire existed on Atlantis. Plato described the founding of Atlantis by Poseidon, god of the sea, and he gave a detailed account of the wealth and splendor of this empire. Plato wrote that the armies of Atlantis planned to subdue the world and were successful in parts of Europe and Africa. The Athenians, however, resisted their attack.

There are many major sites which have been proposed as the actual site of Atlantis. Many people believe that the continent of Atlantis was in the Atlantic Ocean near the Bahamas. In a reading that Edgar Cayce did in 1933, he prophesied that the ruins of Atlantis would soon reappear. He said, "A portion of the temple of Atlantis may yet be discovered under the slime of ages near what is known as Bimini, off the coast of Florida."

In 1968 an underwater structure was discovered on the sea floor near Bimini in the Bahamas. Divers found huge rectangular stones and other architectural features, including eroded marble pillars. Since then, divers have discovered buildings, temples, walls, roads, and whole cities under the water. In 1972, archaeologists and divers off the coast of Bimini discovered buildings and walls which varied from 230 to 812 feet in length. It has been estimated that the weight of a single sixteen-foot-long stone is about twenty-five tons. In deeper water, divers reported sighting what appeared to be a marble citadel or acropolis covering four or five undersea acres, with roads leading from it to unknown destinations.

It is believed that the Atlantians were technologically more advanced than we are today. They knew and used various forms of energy. They understood atomic energy and the use of the laser. They also understood how to control the energy forces within the earth. They used solar energy and massive crystals as a power source. They had powerful weapons of war. Their machinery was far superior to any of our machines, and many operated on solar power. Along with their spacecraft, they had hovercraft which could go over the water as well as over land.

As time passed, the Atlantians became less and less spiritual and more mercenary. Those of the ruling class, for the most part, were self-centered and cruel. The government leaders had great power over the people and ruled them by fear. They imposed a caste system in which the lowest class were like slaves and were mistreated.

The Atlantian scientists used their superior knowledge of DNA to clone workers for specific tasks. They believed that the clones they created were not human but merely animals. Some of the clones were used to provide body parts for the people in the higher castes. The scientists also produced an assortment of strange animals through the process of artificial insemination, using human sperm placed in the wombs of animals. Some of their experiments resulted in beautiful animals, but most were misshapen and ugly. The scientists deliberately bred strong horses that were intelligent and could labor hard and long in the fields. When these strange animals mated, even stranger results were obtained. The spiritual Atlantians declared that the clones and the half-human beings had the spirit of God within their cells, and therefore they were human and not animals. But the people no longer listened to the counsel of the priests and priestesses.

Families began to fall apart as the Atlantians became

more and more sexually degenerate. There were orgies as people sought new thrills. Some of the people craved sex with the various animals. Edgar Cayce refers to the half-human beings who were the result of cohabitation between the Atlantians and the animals as "Things." There are those who believe that the original sin of Earthians was cohabitating with animals.

Most of the people of that time felt that these Things were no better than the beasts of the field, but there were a few who regarded them as human and argued that they had Souls and brains and should be given every opportunity to develop their potential. In some of the temples, cosmetic surgery was performed on the half-human beings to remove remnants of tails, long ears, or misshapen noses.

The Planetary Lords became upset over the degenerate, sexual behavior of the Atlantians and decided that each animal should be restricted to reproducing only its own kind. The Higher Beings agreed that the destruction of Atlantis was necessary not only to destroy the Things but also to get rid of the negativity that the Atlantians had created. One myth relates that Zeus decided to punish Atlantis when the citizens began to behave themselves "unseemly," so he caused their country to sink below the waters.

It is believed that when Atlantis sank there was a great loss of life and huge destruction which affected other land masses as well. If Atlantis was situated on the mid-Atlantic ridge, it could certainly have sunk, because this is one of the world's most active earthquake belts. There are also constant undersea volcanic disturbances which change the depth and topography of the ocean bottom, causing islands to appear and disappear.

Before the final destruction of Atlantis, the priests and priestesses gathered together their followers, along with those who were on the spiritual path, and departed.

They took with them their superior knowledge and their advanced machinery. Some went to the east and settled in the area known as Egypt. Others went west and settled in what is now known as Mexico and Central and South America. Today many of the spiritual survivors from Atlantis are incarnating in America. Once again their voices are being raised in a warning regarding cloning and the necessity of putting spiritual values first.

It is believed that the Atlantians were the first to build pyramids, which they used for their initiations as well as for meditation centers. They understood the great power within a pyramid and spent time inside in order to replenish their energy field. When the spiritual people left Atlantis, they took with them the laser equipment and levitation tools needed to build pyramids in their new colonies.

Historians are puzzled because there are civilizations that did not evolve but suddenly burst into being, almost as if they had been imported from some other country. Which, of course, is exactly what did occur. When the technically advanced Atlantian colonists settled in their new countries, they brought with them their tools and engineering techniques, as well as their knowledge of medicine and science. They built great cities with enormous temples, colossal statues, and pyramids of overwhelming size. After this first burst of civilization, they did not seem to develop much further, and as generations passed they eventually retrogressed. This is what happened in Egypt as well as in Central and South America.

Three civilizations arose in Mexico, Central and South America: the Maya of Yucatan, the Toltec/Aztec of Mexico, and the pre-Inca and Inca of Peru. As time passed, the Planetary Lords began to observe that many of the people were being influenced more by Earth's negativity than by the positive vibrations of love. Word was sent out for volunteers who would be willing to come to Earth and help educate and guide the people of Earth. Some of these Masters came from our solar system, and some came from distant star systems. These Avatars came to various groups of people to teach them the Truth.

The Mayas, Aztecs, and Incas all had legends in common. They told of bearded white men who came to their country who had remarkable abilities and taught peace and brotherhood. Their leader was a wise and powerful Master whom the Aztecs called Quetzalcoatl and the Maya called Kukulkan.

Aztec legend referred to the Toltecs as ancient heroes who brought civilization to Mexico. The Toltecs built a capital named Tula. One of their temples was dedicated to the Plumed Serpent, Quetzalcoatl, the founder of Tula. Eventually, nomadic tribes overthrew the Toltec empire and founded the Aztec empire, but Quetzalcoatl remained the major god of both the Toltec and Aztec. The Aztec historians remembered Quetzalcoatl as the great priest-king of Tula who was wise, kind, and humane. He was a teacher of the arts, lawgiver, master builder, and merciful judge. Quetzalcoatl came to Mexico with his astronomers, mathematicians, artists, and builders. He taught that the divine powers required no sacrifices of either men or animals, but rather offerings of fruit or flowers.

The most ancient Maya legends related that the earliest cities were built by bearded white men who came in the Great Arrival from the sea. These Avatars taught the Mayan people mathematics and astronomy and reorganized the calendar. The Maya became the world's greatest mathematicians and could calculate precise dates for hundreds of thousands of years. Mayan legend also tells of the great god Kukulkan, who came from an unknown country wearing a white robe. He came as a missionary, lawgiver, doctor, and adviser on many practical aspects of life. He taught the people the sciences and the arts. Under the guidance of Kukulkan, the Maya enjoyed peace and prosperity. Legends say that when Kukulkan had fulfilled his mission he boarded a flying ship which took him to the morning star. Kukulkan left the Mayans with wise laws and a rich heritage.

The legends of the pre-Inca people say that the stars were inhabited and that the gods came down from the stars and went back to them. They traveled through the heavens in fireships and possessed terrifying weapons. One legend tells the story of a group of settlers who came to Earth from Venus. Because Venus was closer to the Sun, her seas began to dry up and what little fauna and flora remained were dying. So the Venusians prepared to move away from their planet. They built vast mother ships to ferry the people from their planet to Earth, which was their nearest neighbor. Many of these highly intelligent Venusians settled in the area now known as Peru. Some of the Incas may be descendants of these space people. The colonists remained in South America until a great upheaval occurred which resulted in the Andes being pushed up, causing the once fertile plains to become barren and mountainous.

Archaeological traces of this civilization still remain. Near the ancient Inca fortress of Cuzco are enormous buildings which existed long before the Inca fortress of the Sun God was built. These pre-Inca structures give the impression of being constructed with the most advanced technical skill. The granite blocks have accurately cut grooves and show signs of being exposed to tremendously high temperatures. Archaeologists have yet to discover by what method this great complex was built. They are also unable to determine the date or the people involved in the construction.

Near the ancient Peruvian city of Nazca is a strip of level land about thirty-seven miles long and a mile wide. On this plain gigantic roads are laid out geometrically. Some roads run parallel to each other while others intersect. There are archaeologists who believe that these are ancient Inca roads. However, this seems unlikely not only because they run parallel to each other but because they end abruptly. It is more likely that they were runways built by the Venusians where they could land their spacecraft.

The time came when the Venusians decided to leave Earth because of the harsh climate. Their scouts discovered Proxima Centauri, which is a star similar to the Sun but older and more stable. Proxima Centauri is 4.3 light years away from Earth, which would seem to indicate that it would take thousands of terrestrial years of cosmic flight to reach this solar system. However, physicists and astronomers actually confirm that the speed of light is not the upper limit of all motion. In fact, spaceships could be in any desired place without time passing, because they are not flying in linear time but traveling in the higher dimensions where there exists only the eternal now. The Venusians, like all extraterrestrials, also had available enormous amounts of energy. All this made it possible to fly to another solar system in a very short time. When the Venusians departed, they left some of their people here on Earth to help advance the knowledge and consciousness of the Earthians.

Because the survivors of Atlantis built similar pyramids in Egypt, Mexico, and Central and South America, it has made it a little easier to trace our ancestry back to ancient times. From Mexico to Peru, the colonists built massive pyramids, temples, and palaces. In the jungles of

Mexico alone there may be hundreds of pyramids still waiting to be uncovered. Most of the pyramids of pre-Columbian times probably served a religious purpose and were built as temples.

Since my high school days I've been fascinated with pyramids. My first opportunity to explore a pyramid was many years ago during Easter vacation. I took the twenty-five-mile bus ride from my hotel in Mexico City to the pyramids of the Sun and Moon at Teotihuacan. The Pyramid of the Sun is so big it was really difficult to take it all in. Although this pyramid is only about two-thirds the height of the Great Pyramid in Egypt, it covers a considerably greater area. The oldest text about Teotihuacan tells that the gods assembled here even before Earthians existed. According to an ancient legend, a woman called Oryana arrived in a golden spaceship from the stars with the purpose of building a city at Teotihuacan and producing Earthly rulers. When she had completed her mission, she returned to the stars.

Several years after visiting the pyramids at Teotihuacan, I found myself riding a temperamental camel on my way from Cairo to see the Great Pyramid in Gizeh. I was disappointed that, through the ages, the limestone facing of the pyramid had been removed to be used for buildings in Cairo. With a sense of déja vu, I remembered how the original stone facing had once made this pyramid shine as brightly as the Sun.

The three pyramids at Gizeh are the largest and best preserved of all the Egyptian pyramids. The Great Pyramid was built very early in Egypt's history and ranks as one of man's most spectacular achievements. Its base covers an area large enough to hold ten football fields. It is about forty-five stories high and contains more than two and one-half million stone blocks weighing up to twelve tons each. It is believed that these gigantic blocks were cut out of the quarries using advanced laser tools. Then the blocks were transported and put into place using giant levitation machines. The blocks were fitted together to the nearest thousandth of an inch. Even today we do not have the machines or equipment to build a replica of this pyramid.

The day after I saw the pyramids at Gizeh, I took a tour bus to see the step pyramid south of Cairo at the site of the ancient city of Saqqara. It is believed that Imhotep, a great physician and architect, built this first known pyramid for King Zoser around 2650 B.C. Thirty-five other pyramids still stand near the Nile River in Egypt. Most of these were built as burial places for the pharaohs. Even though some archaeologists say that the Great Pyramid was also built as a sepulchre, others believe that the empty red granite sarcophagus in the King's Chamber was never meant to be a burial place, but rather a place of initiation.

It was several years later that I had the opportunity to see the pyramids in the Yucatán Peninsula, especially the one at Chichén Itzá. A friend and I joined a group touring the Yucatán Peninsula. We had spent several days in Merida and were traveling by bus to Chichén Itzá. It was midmorning by the time our group reached Chichén Itzá. After receiving our room assignments in a beautiful hacienda that had been converted into a hotel, we walked down a shady pathway leading to the Mayan ruins. As our tour guide led the others to one of the more distant structures, I sat in the welcome shade of a large oak tree on a flat rock that might have been, in ages past, part of a Mayan altar. For awhile, I watched as tourists braved the steep steps leading to the top of the great pyramid. Then I closed my eyes and almost immediately felt the presence of someone sitting beside me.

Then I heard within my head these words: *Welcome to our sacred place.*

I was startled and asked mentally, "Who are you?"

You may call me "Spinner of Tales," he replied, *for I have within my remembrance all the stories of my people from ancient times until now.*

"Tell me, then, of the ancient times," I requested.

At the beginning of time, related Spinner of Tales, *our people were but humble peasants who went about their daily tasks of gathering and preparing food with little enthusiasm or purpose of life. Then there came from a far-off place a flying ship carrying tall, shining gods. These gods brought with them great mysteries which they shared with my people. They taught us their language so we could communicate. They brought us a number system and knowledge of the stars. They told us of the beauty of their faraway home.*

The gods trained some of our people in astrology and astronomy. They showed others how to use their tools of magic to cut through rock and lift these heavy stones into place as easily as lifting a small pebble. Together we built this great pyramid as a special place where god and peasant might sing praises to the highest god, Kukulkan.

The gods trained some of my people in the art of healing, showing them which herbs to use and how to administer them. Others were trained to use their powers to foretell the future. Some chose to become priests, and to them were revealed even greater mysteries. They were told how the gods created humans who were the ancestors of our people the Mayans. So we are the children of the gods and it was good that once again they came to give to us much wisdom. Our ceremonies here at this sacred place are to give thanks to the gods for rain, for abundance, and most of all for life.

For a long time, I sat with my eyes closed. When I finally opened my eyes, the Spinner of Tales was gone. Later, when my friend joined me in the shade of the oak tree, I tried to explain to her what I had just experienced, but she found it difficult to believe or to understand. Personally, I shall always remember my meeting with the Spinner of Tales in Chichén Itzá.

At Copan and Palenque, as well as at Chichén Itzá, the Mayans built beautiful temples and large pyramids. Then around 600 A.D., for no apparent reason, the inhabitants left their solidly built cities, with their rich temples, artistic pyramids, and grand stadiums. The inhabitants never returned, and gradually the jungle grew back and turned everything into a vast landscape of ruins.

Tracing our ancestry is difficult because much of the ancient literature has been destroyed, either intentionally or by chance. The ancient books were long parchment or papyrus scrolls which were kept in libraries in large cities. When Alexander the Great conquered the Persian Empire, the library in the capital was burned. The Romans burned the library in Carthage. Omar, the third caliph of Islam, burned the library of Alexandria. The emperor of China in the third century b.c. ordered all books to be burned except those that dealt with medicine or agriculture. When Bishop Diego de Landa came to the Yucatán, he destroyed all the Mayan writings he could find. The Egyptians even used ancient manuscripts as mummy wrappings.

The recorded history that we do have has survived because it was cut in stone, inscribed on seals, baked in clay tablets, or painted on temple or tomb walls. Other knowledge has survived in the form of legends or myths which have been passed down from generation to generation. Some believe that a few ancient manuscripts still survive and are hidden in several places, including the Sphinx and the Vatican. Stored in the Vatican Library is the world's most important collection of early manuscripts. Included in the more than 50,000 valuable ancient manuscripts are many of Roman, Greek, and Oriental origin. Currently there are plans to make copies of some of the manuscripts available to scholars. If the contents of these manuscripts are revealed, we will be able to learn more about our ancient ancestors.

10

Guidance from Above

Physical
Energy
Emotional
Soul

Conscious
Unconscious
Subconscious
Superconscious

The Higher Beings knew how difficult it would be to live in the physical world with its duality of good and evil. They knew that we who incarnated on Earth would need a Heavenly Father/Mother who would be our constant companion, advisor, and friend. So whether we are aware of it or not, we all have a Higher Self who is the most important Master in our life.

How can we know someone we have never physically seen or heard or felt? Through faith, we can know that our Higher Self is always with us to give counsel and to protect us. By faith, we know that our Higher Self is our spiritual partner who loves us more than we can even comprehend. Through meditation, we can intuitively listen to our Higher Self. Through prayer we can communicate with our Higher Self. Our Higher Self is not only known as our Twin Soul or Twin Flame, but also as Master, Christ, and God Self. Without the help of our Higher Self, we would not be able to achieve enlightenment.

Sometimes when we first become acquainted with our Higher Self, we may feel that it is important that we know his name. I asked many times, and finally my Higher Self told me I could call him "David," which means "Beloved One." Over the course of all our lifetimes on Earth, we have had many different names. At the same time, we have had only one eternal name by which we are identified in the Higher Realms. This name is made up of musical tones rather than spoken sounds. This is probably why it would be difficult for us to express the true name of the Higher Self even if we were made aware of it.

Our Higher Self, like all of the Higher Beings, is androgynous, both male and female. The English language needs a special pronoun to indicate both male and female. God Almighty deserves to be referred to in a respectful manner, as do all the Higher Beings. It sounds strange to say "it" or "he/she," so until an appropriate pronoun is invented in English, I will use "he" when referring to the Higher Self.

The Higher Self plays many different roles in our life. We might even become confused and feel that there are a lot of different Higher Beings who are involved. But it is the Higher Self who plays the role that we need at any particular time in our life. Some of my clients tell me that they have many guides. My reply is that the Higher Self is so wise and all-knowing that there is no one in the whole world better able to be our guide.

When we are children, our Higher Self plays the role of Guardian Angel and spiritual mother, guiding, protecting, and watching over us. As we grow older, we begin to realize how important the Higher Self is in our life. He becomes our friend and confidant. We also recognize the fact that the Higher Self is not only our partner in the spiritual portion of our lives, but in our daily life and career as well.

The Higher Self is our best friend. Nobody in the whole universe cares for us as much as our own Higher Self. When we are lonely, we can reach out with our hearts to our Higher Self and ask to be surrounded with his love. There may be a time when our family or friends have let us down or have disappointed us. We can always depend upon the love of our Higher Self. No matter what happens, our Higher Self will never disappoint us, will never let us down, will never stop loving us.

As we become more aware of our Higher Self, we will be able to work closely together as partners and friends. This is a true partnership. Just as we need our Higher Self, our Higher Self needs us. Only through us can he express in the physical world. The Higher Self is the intermediary between God and us. As we continue to mature spiritually, more of the power of the Holy Spirit will flow to us through our Higher Self.

Since our first life on Earth, we have been partners with our Higher Self. While we are living our life in the physical world, our Higher Self is living his life in a higher dimension. Because the Higher Self has never incarnated into a physical body, he has not become entangled in karmic debts, and thus he has remained in a state of perfection. Therefore, our Higher Self is a perfect, personal role model who can serve as a pattern for our life.

In the past, when people desired to become enlightened, they had to find a wise guru or spiritual teacher to help them on their path. In the present age, we no longer need to hunt for a spiritual guru, because the Higher Self is a wise teacher and our spiritual guide who is always ready to give us advice and knowledge. Other sources of information are also available to help us along our spiritual path; there are video and cassette tapes, books, classes and lectures. Each may have something that will be of help to us. But *discernment* is very important, because the personal prejudices or opinions of the author might color the Truth.

When we become enlightened, we will have attained the high state of Christ consciousness. The term "Christ" is a title of achievement and is the equivalent of the word "Master." We recognize the fact that Jesus is indeed a Master when we speak of him as "Jesus the Christ." There are many people who look to Jesus the Christ the way others look to the Higher Self for guidance, protection, and love. This does not bother the Higher Self because he is used to playing many roles. When referring to our Higher Self, the terms "Christ Self" and "Master Self" are synonymous. The most exalted name for our Higher Self is "God Self." This recognizes the fact that the essence of God is a part of our Higher Self, just as the Holy Spirit is a part of our own being.

For eons, Masters have been coming down to Earth to different groups of people to teach them a better way of life and help them achieve enlightenment. These Avatars are highly trained and dedicated men and women who make their appearance in various parts of the world when and where they are needed. Their purpose is to help humanity. They teach, advise, and set an example for the people. Their very presence has a beneficial effect on humanity. Quetzalcoatl came to the Aztecs. Kukulkan came to the Maya. Other Masters came to other races and groups of people. Some of these Avatars were well received and held in high esteem. Others were killed by the very people they had come to help.

Jesus the Christ came to the Jewish people in Palestine. Many believed that he was the Messiah they were expecting. His message was of God's love for humanity. He also stressed the importance of brotherly love. Christian beliefs are based on the teachings of Jesus. Christianity is the most widespread religion in the world.

Gautama Buddha was the Master who founded Buddhism in India. Buddha taught that religion should be devoid of authority, ritual, and tradition. Instead it should be an individual growth experience. The Buddhist goal in life is to reach Nirvana, a state of complete peace and love.

Confucius came as a Master to China and was the founder of Confucianism. He taught benevolence and love for all people. Some consider Confucianism a system of ethics rather than a religion, because Confucius taught more about how people should act toward one another than about God. Confucius, however, did believe in a Supreme Being, called Shang Ti.

Muhammad came to Arabia and founded the religion of Islam. Muhammad, which means "Praised One," became one of the most influential men of all time. His followers, the Muslims, believe there is one God, Allah, and that Muhammad was his prophet. The Koran records Allah's revelations to Muhammad. The word "Islam" means "peace through submission to God."

Tradition says that Lao Tzu, the Old Master, founded Taoism in China. The sacred book of Taoism stresses a way of life that is serene, happy and in harmony with nature. It considers humility one of the highest virtues.

Zoroaster came to the Persians and was the founder of Zoroastrianism. The religion centers around the god of righteousness and light, Ahura Mazda. Most of his followers, known as Parsis, now live in India.

The Baha'i Faith was founded by a Persian called Baha'u'llah. The Baha'is believe that God sent many prophets to teach moral truths: their prophets include Abraham, Jesus, and Muhammad, and the latest Master, Baha'u'llah. He believed that all religions honor the same God and that the highest form of worship is service to others.

These Masters came with a message of love and brotherhood. As time passed, however, some of their followers began to impose their own interpretations on the teachings of their Master. Now it seems that many of the followers of the various religions not only distorted the message of these Masters but began to feel that their way was the only path to enlightenment and to God.

It was a common belief among ancient peoples, including those in the Orient, Egypt, and Palestine, that many of the Masters and Avatars were divinely conceived. They believed that these great Masters were born into the physical plane by what has been termed a "virgin birth," whereby sperm of a Higher Being was placed in the womb of a physical woman. According to tradition, Lao Tzu, who wrote one of the basic books of the Chinese Taoism philosophy was born of a virgin. The Master Gautama, founder of Buddhism, was also believed to have been begotten by God and born to a virgin whose name was Maya.

One of the main gods of Hinduism is Vishnu. The Hindus believe that Vishnu sometimes incarnates into a physical body when Earth is faced with a catastrophe or when mankind needs comfort and guidance. One of the incarnations was Krishna, who was born of a virgin named Devaki. She was chosen because of her purity to become the mother of God. Cyrus, King of Persia, was also believed to have been of divine origin. In the records of his time, he was referred to as the anointed Son of God.

Probably the greatest Master was the one we call Jesus, who came to the people in Israel. When an angel told Mary she would give birth to a son, she asked the angel, "How can this be, since I am a virgin?" The angel said to her, "The Holy Spirit will come upon you, and the power of the Highest will overshadow you; therefore, that Holy One who is to be born will be called the Son of God."

Many of the great Masters had a special experience in their lives, a time of enlightenment, when they became aware of who they were and what their mission was to be. The Master Muhammad was in his thirties when he had a vision of the angel Gabriel, who called him to be a prophet and proclaim God's message to his countrymen in Arabia.

For many years Gautama searched for enlightenment. Finally, one day as he was meditating under a shady bodhi tree, he reached his goal of enlightenment and he became aware of his mission on Earth. His followers gave him the title "Buddha," which means "Enlightened One."

When it was time for Jesus to begin his public ministry at the age of thirty, he went to the Jordan River to be baptized by John. As Jesus came up out of the water, the heavens were opened and the Spirit of God came down in the form of a dove. A voice from heaven said, "This is my beloved Son, and I am wonderfully pleased with him."

When Masters reach the close of their public ministry on Earth, they lay down their physical bodies through death. Because they have already achieved Mastership, they do not need to enter the Astral World. They ascend to the Higher Realms and dwell in their soul bodies. Ancient writings relate that after Krishna was crucified, he ascended into Heaven. At the time of his ascension, a great light enveloped Krishna and he disappeared into the light. The records show that Buddha's last appearance was on top of a mountain in the presence of his followers. Buddha's followers claim that as he rose to the celestial regions a great light surrounded him, and he disappeared into the light.

After Jesus was crucified, Joseph of Arimathea asked Pilate for permission to take Jesus' body down off the cross. Nicodemus came bringing embalming ointment made from myrrh and aloes. Together, Joseph and Nicodemus wrapped Jesus' body in a long linen cloth saturated with spices, as was the Jewish custom of burial.

Three days after the crucifixion, two of Jesus' disciples came to the tomb. When they looked inside they discovered that Jesus' body was gone, but they saw the linen cloth still lying there. Later, Mary Magdalene was standing outside the tomb crying. As she wept, she stooped and looked in and saw two white-robed angels sitting at the head and foot of the place where the body of Jesus had been lying. They told her that Jesus had risen from the dead.

In his spiritual body, Jesus was able to appear and disappear at will. One evening the disciples were meeting behind locked doors, in fear of the Jewish leaders, when suddenly Jesus was standing among them! After greeting his disciples, he showed them his wounded hands and side. Eight days later the disciples were together again, and this time Thomas was with them. The doors were locked, but suddenly, as before, Jesus was standing among them and greeting them.

There are those who have not understood the resurrection. Some believe that Jesus' physical body had been resurrected. Others believe that Jesus wasn't really dead. It depends on our definition of death. Of course, we are all eternal beings, so we will continue to be alive. However, when we ascend into a higher dimension, the physical body is left behind because it is composed of substances that are compatible only to the Earth plane.

The mystery, then, is what happened to Jesus' physical body? Cosmic tradition tells us that in a tremendous burst of energy Jesus' physical body was completely disintegrated. That may explain the markings on the shroud of Turin, which tradition claims was wrapped around Jesus' body. This linen cloth shows a photographic negative, a reversal of lights and shadows, which could have been caused by intense heat as the body disintegrated. It reveals a life-size front and back figure of a man. The bloody stains indicate that the man had been beaten, lanced, and crucified.

Several weeks after Jesus rose from the dead, he led his disciples out along the road to Bethany. Lifting his hands to heaven, Jesus blessed them, and then he began rising into the sky and disappeared into a cloud, leaving them staring after him.

The religions which the great Masters founded have been a powerful force in the world. There has never been a culture that did not have some form of religion. Millions of people have died for their religious beliefs. Many nations have gone to war in the name of religion. Because we live in a country where we have religious freedom, it may come as a surprise to us that in the 1990s millions of religious believers around the world are being systematically persecuted and killed not only by extremist groups but even by their own governments. As long as Jews, Christians, Muslims, Buddhists, and Baha'is are victims of religious persecution, we are all in danger of losing the priceless gift of religious freedom. It would seem that we have a long way to go before all races and religions can live together in peace.

There are many different names for God and many spiritual paths that lead to enlightenment. Even though we may feel that we have found the best religion, it is not the only religion. We are not to judge others for their religious beliefs. Everyone has the right to his own belief. That is exactly what religious freedom means. Tolerance needs to begin within each and every one of us. Only then can we begin to live together in peace.

As we prepare to enter the 21st century, more and more Masters are incarnating to help us achieve peace on Earth. According to a Jewish legend, there are Masters here on Earth who don't proclaim their Mastership but walk among us unobtrusively. They may be disguised as anyone from a homeless person standing on the street corner to the salesperson at our local department store. Because we might encounter a Master at any moment, we will begin to view humanity from a different perspective. In order not to be rude to a Master, we will begin to treat everyone we contact with love and respect.

Many different religions believe that their particular Master will some day return to Earth. The Christians are looking forward to the second coming of Jesus the Christ. The Jews are expecting their Messiah. The Hindus expect the Avatar of the new age. Buddhists expect the return of Maitreya Buddha. Many believe that a World Teacher will incarnate on Earth. We have been told by the Higher Beings that not just a single Master, but many will cooperate together as World Teachers who will help to guide the people of Earth. We will certainly need the help and guidance of all these Masters if we are to achieve unity and peace on our beautiful planet Earth.

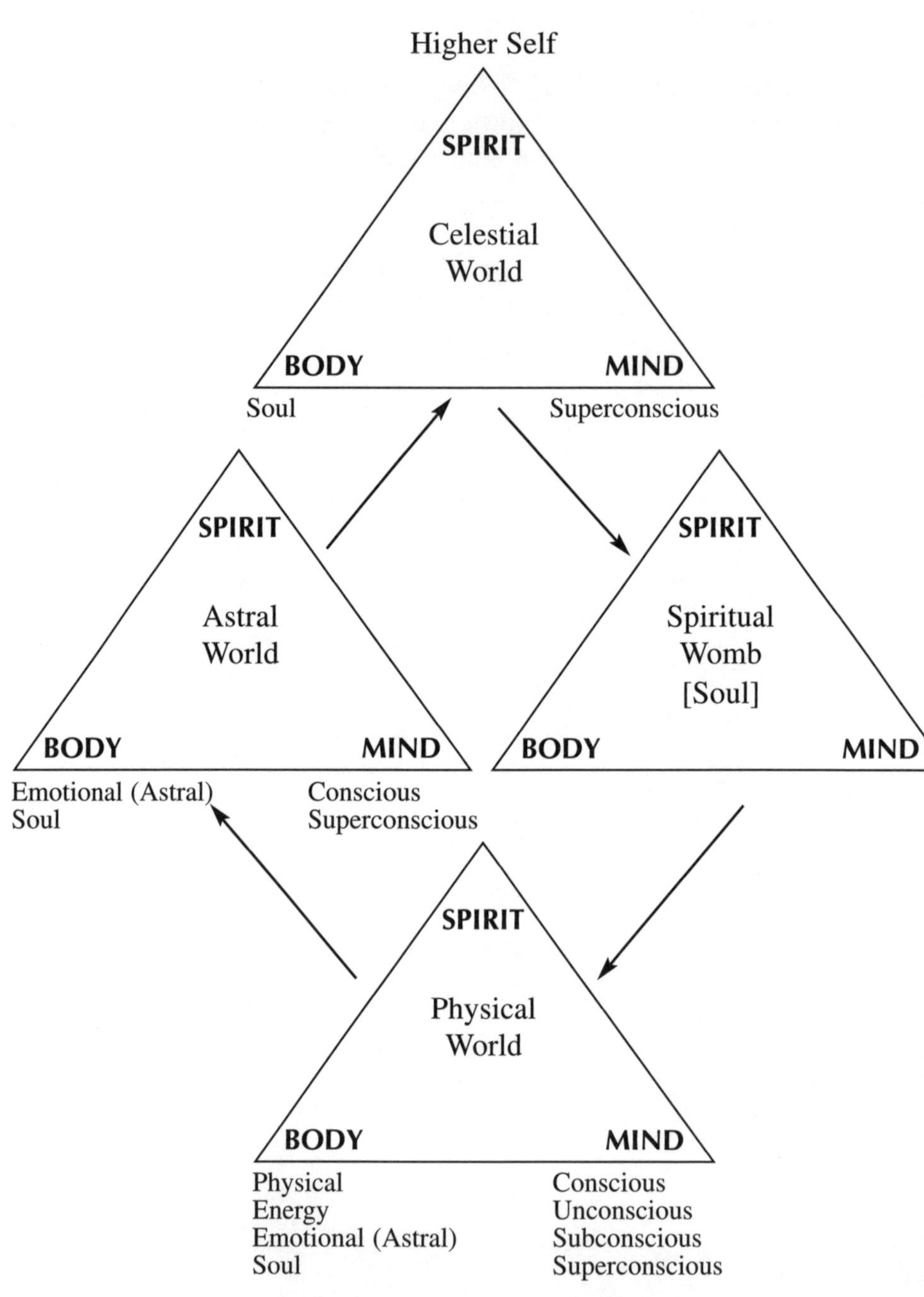

The Cycle of Birth and Rebirth

11

Ending the Cycle of Birth and Rebirth

One summer while vacationing in Israel, I went by bus to the Essene settlement at Khirbat Qumran, which is perched on the hills above the Dead Sea. As I walked among the ruins, the place felt very familiar, as though I had lived here in some long-ago time. I could almost hear the sounds of birds in a dovecote outside my window two thousand years ago. It was here at Qumran that several jars of scrolls were discovered hidden in caves in the steep hillside. These scrolls, the oldest Biblical manuscripts yet found, were copied and hidden by the Essenes to preserve the truth for generations yet to come. There are those who believe that the complete story of the eternal evolution of the Soul will be found in these Dead Sea Scrolls, as well as in the libraries at the Vatican and hidden beneath the Sphinx in Egypt. The whole truth about reincarnation will be revealed in the new age when we are ready to receive it with understanding.

During the time that Jesus was living on Earth, there were three major Jewish religious groups: the Sadducees, the Pharisees, and the Essenes. These three groups represent the attitudes people have even to this day about reincarnation.

The Sadducees were active in Judea until Jerusalem fell in 70 A.D. They accepted only the written law of the Torah, the Jewish scriptures. The Sadducees did not believe in immortality. They said that we live one life and that the Soul dies with the body.

The Pharisees were members of another Jewish sect who lived in Palestine and followed strict laws. They considered themselves more holy and righteous than ordinary people. Jesus called them hypocrites or pretenders. The Pharisees did not believe in reincarnation, but they did believe in life after death.

The Essenes were members of a Jewish sect living in Palestine from 100 B.C. to about 100 A.D. Tradition says that those nearest to Jesus, including his parents and his cousin John, belonged to an Essene group. The Essenes believed that we are eternal beings — that we have lived before and that we will continue to return to Earth until we have learned the lessons of love.

Today there is still a wide range of divergent views among Jewish theologians. Reform Jews have no belief in the immortality of the Soul, except that after death the spirit of a person remains alive in his children and in their memory of him. Orthodox Jews believe that the physical body will be resurrected when the Messiah comes; and the dead will rise from the grave and live again. There are some Jews who believe that the resurrected body and the immortal Soul will, in time, become as one; meanwhile, the spirit lives in another realm waiting for the coming of the Messiah and the resurrection.

It is a matter of historical record that many early Christians believed in reincarnation. Jesus never taught that it was a false belief. He made references to it on several occasions. In Matthew 16:13,14, he asked his disciples, "Who are the people saying I am?"

"Well," they replied, "some say John the Baptist come back to life; some, Elijah; some, Jeremiah or one of the other prophets."

If the concept of reincarnation was prevalent in

early Christian thought, why is it not a part of Christian theology today? Because down through the centuries, most of the references to reincarnation have been deleted from the Bible.

Constantine the Great was the first emperor of Rome to become a Christian. In 325 A.D., he presided over the first General Council of the Christian Church, which met in Nicaea. More than three hundred bishops from all parts of the empire attended. There, in an atmosphere of dissension, jealousy, and intolerance, these religious leaders decided what writings should be included and which should be omitted from the Bible. It is not surprising that under these circumstances a great deal of inspired writing was deliberately omitted, especially that which was concerned with reincarnation and angelic beings. If someone had an opinion contrary to church doctrine, it was declared a crime of heresy. Constantine signed the death warrants of many people — including his own son — who failed to conform to the accepted Church dogma.

During the fifth Ecumenical Council, held in 553 A.D., the belief in reincarnation was banned by a slim margin of votes, and at that time it ceased to be accepted by the Christian religion. The religious leaders of that day felt that the belief in reincarnation would weaken their power and authority. They also rejected the idea of karma — the concept that we reap the results of our actions, whether in this life or in a future one. The decisions made by these men so long ago are still influencing the Catholic and Protestant religions today.

Buddha preached that life is a continuing cycle of death and rebirth. He also taught that karma, the law of action, is the responsibility of each individual and that behavior in a previous life determines the new life. Good deeds may lead to rebirth as someone wealthy and intelligent or even to rebirth in Heaven. Evil deeds may lead to rebirth into poverty and illness, or even to rebirth in Hell. Until a person achieves Nirvana, or total enlightenment, he must be born and reborn many times.

Some people do not believe in reincarnation because they confuse it with the concept of transmigration. The word "transmigration" comes from two words, *trans* meaning "across," and *migrate* meaning "to move." It is the belief that the human Soul is immortal and that after death it returns to Earth in another living body. Sometimes people may be so utterly degenerate in a life that they are not fit to incarnate as a human being and must return in an animal form. This belief prevailed among many ancient people especially in Greece and Egypt. It is still believed by many of the Hindu sects of India.

Hinduism teaches that the Soul never dies. When the body dies, the Soul is reborn. If a person performs honorable deeds and lives a good life, the Soul will be born into a higher state, perhaps into the body of a holy person. If one performs evil deeds and leads a bad life, the Soul will be born into a lower state, perhaps into the body of an animal. Hindus believe that people continue to incarnate until they achieve spiritual perfection. The Soul then enters a new level of existence from which it never returns to Earth.

Reincarnation is the belief that the Soul is immortal and that we incarnate many times, but we return to the physical world only through a human body. The word "reincarnation" comes from *re*, meaning "again," and *carn*, meaning "flesh." When we have achieved enlightenment, we will no longer need to incarnate in a physical body.

There are some who reject the idea of reincarnation and past life regressions as an ego trip, a desire to vicariously experience a life of wealth, fame, and fortune. In the twenty-five years that I have been regressing people, they have usually gone back to lives that are quite ordinary and mundane. However, two men who came to me for past life regressions seemed to be the exceptions.

One day a tall, handsome man came to my office and introduced himself as Bill. He said that he wasn't sure whether or not he believed in reincarnation, but he had an open mind and he wanted me to regress him to a past life. During the regression, he remembered interesting, personal experiences in Abraham Lincoln's life. Here was a well-educated, brilliant man who certainly did not seem out of place having experienced a past life as Lincoln.

Several months later, James, another tall, ruggedly handsome man, came to me for a regression. I knew that he had made quite a name for himself in politics and had even run for president of the United States on the Independent ticket. To my complete surprise, James also regressed to a past life as Abraham Lincoln. However, James seemed stuck in the last events of Lincoln's life — seeing him in his coffin and being moved to tears.

Almost a year later, Bill returned for a second regression. I asked if it would be all right if I took him back to the past life as Lincoln and he agreed. I helped him achieve a very deep alpha state, much deeper than during his first regression. This time the true story came tumbling out. Bill had been a law partner when Lincoln set up his practice in Springfield, Illinois. In that lifetime, the man's name had been William, but Lincoln always called him Billy.

Many months later, I met James at a party, and I offered to regress him to his life as Lincoln again to discover more details. He agreed, and I put him in a much deeper alpha state than before. This time a completely different story came to the surface. James had been an officer in charge of protecting President Lincoln. One night, when Lincoln decided to see a play at Ford's Theater, James had assigned two other officers to protect the president. James was across the street drinking when the president was shot. James blamed himself because he felt that he could have prevented the tragedy if he had been by Lincoln's side that night.

When someone relives a life as a famous person, it may not be exactly as they pictured it to be. Instead of a life as Cleopatra, it may have been a life as her handmaiden. After all, it isn't who we were in a past life that is important — it is how well we are learning our lessons in the present life.

It's not necessary for us to know our past lives to become enlightened. In fact, we don't even need to believe in reincarnation. What is required is to live a life of unconditional love.

There are some who say that if there is such a thing as reincarnation, then why are past lives not remembered? The Truth is that when we are born into a physical body our mind is veiled so that we cannot remember our past lives. Indeed, this is a blessing because we have enough challenges in the present life without dragging along our past problems. However, almost everyone at one time or another has met a person or visited a new place and felt an eerie sense of reliving a past experience, the feeling of déja vu. This may be as close as most of us get to remembering our past lives.

Many years ago I was with a tour group going up the Nile in a boat with dirty, patched sails and an even dirtier native guide. As we made our way slowly upriver, I began to have intuitive flashes of a past life when I had been a priestess serving in a beautiful Egyptian temple. As we rounded a bend in the river, our guide pointed out the ruins of a temple — the temple that I had remembered. It was exciting for me to have confirmation of that past life memory.

When we are traveling in a new place, sometimes déja vu takes us by surprise. But at other times, we need to tune into our emotional reaction to a particular place and be sensitive to our inner knowing.

Reincarnation and karma go hand in hand. The word karma in the original Sanskrit means "deed." The Law of Karma states that every thought, word, or action, no matter how small it may be, influences our life. It is cause and effect in action. Karma isn't something mystical. It is a natural law that basically creates for us lessons to learn as a result of our actions in this and previous lives. The learning process involved in karma implies that we have unfinished business with others, as well as with ourselves, and that we are each personally responsible for our every action and thought. We create both positive and negative karma every moment of our lives by the choices we make and the decisions we reach. We and we alone are responsible for everything that happens to us. We have created the reality that we are now experiencing.

Sometimes we may find ourselves in a situation where the reaction to an experience is almost immediate. I call this "instant karma." For example, a car speeds by us on the freeway, cutting in and out of traffic. Several miles down the road, we pass this same driver pulled over by the side of the freeway, receiving a ticket from a policeman. That's instant karma! More often, though, the karma is delayed in this life; it can even be postponed several lifetimes until the right set of circumstances occurs and the person is better prepared to face the learning experience.

Positive karma is the result of patience, understanding, kindliness, love, devotion, hard work, generosity, and concern. When we plant these seeds, we reap health, happiness, and prosperity. Our natural talents — art, music, or sports — which we bring with us into a new life usually relate to talents we have developed in past lives. When we enjoy a harmonious, fulfilling relationship, we may indeed have found our soul mate, whom we have grown to love in previous lifetimes. Often a position of influence and leadership is earned by experiences in other lifetimes. Physical beauty, a loving nature, and an intelligent mind may also be the result of karma we have accumulated in past lifetimes.

Negative karma is generated by greed, intemperance, neglect, jealousy, and hatred in all its forms. When these seeds are sown, the harvest is illness, sorrow, handicaps, and poverty. All the negative seeds we have sown must be harvested in due season. It is a waste of time to lament over the reaping when it is painful. We may as well take care of our karmic debts now rather than at a future time, since they cannot be avoided.

Sooner or later we shall all have to learn the Law of Karma: we must reap what we have sown. Both the positive and negative effects we are reaping now are a result of our actions in this lifetime as well as in previous lifetimes. The seeds we are sowing now will bring forth their effects in either this or a future lifetime.

A negative event or situation that occurs in our life is really an opportunity to learn a lesson and cancel out a karmic debt. The event itself is not that important; what is important is how we react to the event. If we respond in a positive way and learn our lesson, the karmic debt is paid. If we react to the lesson in a negative way, with bitterness, revenge, or anger, we can end up with additional karma to resolve. Learning our lessons means more than just feeling sorry and vowing not to repeat our errors. The test is whether, under the same circumstances and with the same opportunity, we would repeat our mistake. Eventually we will begin to realize that we are not punished *for* our sins but *by* them. If we have not learned our lesson, sometime in the future we will again encounter this same situation. Karma has all the time in the world to continue to try to educate us.

After many years regressing people, I'm beginning to see a pattern unfolding. People who are overweight often suffered and died of starvation in a past life, or they were in a situation where there was a very limited amount of food. Unexplained abdominal pains might be related to a past life incident in which the person was stabbed or shot in the stomach. Sometimes emotional problems or depression can be traced back to a tragedy with strong guilt associations. Headaches may relate to a past life in which one died of a head injury, perhaps by being clubbed, guillotined, or hanged. However, we need to be careful that we don't blame a past life for all our physical problems. We must understand that we are creating karma all the time. Pains in the stomach may result from an ulcer that is the result of emotional stress in the present life.

We cannot change what has happened to us in the past, but the present and future will be determined by the thoughts and choices of today. It really makes no difference whether the physical problem is the result of a cellular memory from a past life or the result of an imbalance in the present life. Whatever the cause, we need to ask our Higher Self for healing, claim that healing, and let the problem go with love.

The belief in reincarnation helps to explain some of our deep-seated fears and phobias. Fresh out of college with a degree in psychology, I thought I knew a great deal about phobias. I knew that a phobia is a recurrent, persistent, often intense fear of some idea, situation, or external object. I knew that just reassuring a person that the phobia is unrealistic accomplishes little or nothing to ease the fear. If we remain in a fearful situation, we may become agitated and even overwhelmed by panic. One of the reasons I knew all this was that I had experienced the anxiety of a phobia since I was a young child.

My phobia has to do with blood. In a classroom, if the teacher just talked about blood, I began to perspire and feel that I was going to faint. In church, if the minister talked about the blood of Jesus, I had to get up and leave. It finally got so bad that wherever I went, I had to sit in an aisle seat near a doorway just in case someone mentioned blood and I had to leave. During a regression, I learned that I had been stabbed by someone I trusted and had slowly bled to death. In the present life, I nearly died from internal hemorrhaging. Little by little I've learned how to handle my phobia, but I'm still not entirely free of my fear.

There is a long list of phobias. There is agoraphobia, the fear of a large open space, and claustrophobia, the fear of confined spaces. Other types of phobias involve sharp instruments, high places, cats, thunderstorms, germs, animals, and the dark. Then there is phobophobia, the fear of fear! My psychology professor said that even though a person may not be consciously aware of the original fear, it probably stemmed from an event that had occurred in early childhood and had been repressed and forgotten. However, the longer I have worked with clients, the more I realize that many phobias did not originate in the present life but during a time of trauma in a past life. And what could be more traumatic than someone's death? Often when I regress clients and take them back to a past life, amazing scenarios begin to unfold.

Kathy came to me because of her extreme fear of birds. She feared being outside because a bird might fly near her. She was even afraid of a bird in a cage. When I regressed her, she returned to a life when she was an Indian woman. The elders of the tribe believed that she had been unfaithful to her mate and they had decided on her punishment. They took her to the top of a mountain, laid her down, and tied her hands and feet so that she was unable to move. There the elders left her to die. Several vultures circled above her for awhile, their wings flapping in the Indian maiden's face. Then the huge birds settled down and began eating her flesh while she still lived. The terror and pain of this experience were indelibly imprinted on Kathy's subconscious mind. Once Kathy understood where her phobia originated, she could start the healing process. Soon she was able to put her hand in my parakeet's cage and let him fly around and light on her finger. Understanding her past life helped Kathy face and overcome her fear of birds.

It is important that we do not judge anyone else's karma, for we do not know the reason why they have chosen certain lessons to learn. We may not know why a wonderful, loving person becomes paralyzed from the waist down as the result of an accident. We may not understand why someone we know is struggling with poor health or financial difficulties, or the loss of a loved one through death or divorce. We may not know why bad things happen to good people, or why we would choose to experience something painful in our life. But when we leave the physical world and enter the next dimension, our questions will be answered and we will understand.

Karma is so orderly and precise that cosmic justice is always guaranteed even though earthly justice may not always be fair. A man may be sentenced to fifteen years in prison for a rape he did not commit. It may appear that an innocent man is being unfairly punished, and yet, for some reason, he drew this experience into his life. Another man kills his ex-wife and the jury finds him not guilty. It seems that he got away with murder, but karmic justice is absolutely foolproof. All karmic debts must be paid, either now or later.

Besides personal karma, there is also group karma. We tend to incarnate with the same people life after life, and we develop merits and demerits as a group. Group karma is created by our association with other people. It operates in every aspect of life — with our social and business associates as well as with family members. Before we incarnated, with the help of our Higher Self, we chose the family in which we would be born. If some of our family members are difficult to get along with, we need to remind ourselves that we chose this particular family group for a reason. In this lifetime, we may have been drawn back together again to take care of a karmic debt that needs to be repaid. We will continue to incarnate until all our relationships have been resolved with unconditional love.

There is also national karma. This can be a blessing or a hindrance. Some of the nations of Africa and Europe are adversely affected by their national karma at this time. In class, I'm often asked why untold thousands of Africans are dying from starvation, illness, and civil uprisings. My answer is that as a nation there are evidently karmic lessons to learn. We will probably not understand what these lessons are until we arrive in a higher dimension. Any nation that goes to war produces karmic debts. The magnitude of this karma is directly connected with the underlying intent of that nation's aggression.

Because of the Law of Karma, we cannot escape our problems by killing ourselves. No matter how despondent we may become, we should not consider suicide as the solution for our problems, because it will only result in additional unhappiness, misery, and pain. What is the karmic debt that must be repaid when someone commits suicide? Each individual case needs to be considered separately. The fact that a person was not able to think clearly because he was under the influence of drugs or alcohol, or because of a mental or emotional problem, is taken into consideration. Committing suicide does not eliminate the problems of life but causes even more negative karma. All work that was left undone, all lessons that were unlearned, all pain that was not experienced must be faced in another lifetime. Added to that is the fact that the person who takes his own life is held responsible for all the agony and emotional distress the suicide caused family and friends.

In this lifetime, I chose to take care of a long-standing debt incurred when I took my own life. One quiet Sunday afternoon, I intuitively tuned into a past life as a gypsy in Spain sometime in the sixteenth century. In my mind, I saw my covered, wooden wagon that I had decorated with brightly colored pictures. Inside the wagon I had made myself a cozy place in which to live. I earned my living by giving card readings in the villages I visited. I preferred to travel alone and I was never lonely. My companion was an old, obedient horse that I had raised from a colt.

On this particular day, I was traveling through the woods to another village when the wagon bounced over a tree root, and I was thrown to the ground. The iron wheel ran over my leg and crushed my kneecap. The pain was unbearable. For several days, I hobbled around leaning on a stick for support. Finally, I could no longer stand the pain. I had no gun or poison, and I didn't want to cut myself and bleed to death, so I had to figure out some other way to kill myself. Finally I settled on a plan. I hitched up my faithful horse and tied one end of a long scarf to the spokes of the wheel and the other end around my neck. Then I tied myself to the seat at the front of the wagon. As I urged my horse forward, the wheels of the wagon went round and round, and the scarf became tighter and tighter until I could no longer breathe. Even as I died, I was pleased that I had found a way to be released from my pain. Luckily, no one else was negatively affected by my death.

A few months later, my Higher Self informed me that within the week I would be in an accident that would settle the karmic debt I had incurred when I committed suicide so long ago. It's a strange feeling waiting for something to happen and not knowing what it will be.

My mother was terminally ill and I had just left her hospital room after feeding her lunch when I slipped and fell. I screamed in agony because of the severity of the pain. An ambulance took me to another hospital, where X-rays showed that I had a broken ankle. However, even when I complained about the pain, they did nothing for my knee, which was dislocated. Eventually my ankle healed, but I was still in a wheelchair because I was unable to bend my knee and any movement caused me severe pain. A year later, after months of therapy and two operations on my knee, I was able to walk across my living room using only two canes to keep my balance. It hadn't been easy, but I had finally taken care of my karmic debt.

Even though karma is a predetermined set of conditions, it is subject to change. Forgiveness is often the only way to stop negative karma. We can ask the person whom we have hurt for his forgiveness, or we can ask our Higher Self for forgiveness. This is where amazing grace comes onto the scene. Grace is a form of spiritual love that forgives us the error of our ways when we acknowledge our faults. Our Higher Self not only forgives but also forgets, so that we have no karmic debt to repay. It is up to us to accept this forgiveness and to love ourselves unconditionally even when we feel that we are not living up to our full potential.

None of us is perfect, and no one knows our faults and foibles better than we do. When we do the best that we can and still fall short of our goal of perfection, it's because we live in an imperfect world. Even the Masters find it difficult to follow a perfect path when they incarnate on Earth. When we reach the place in our spiritual evolvement where we understand the truth of the Law of Grace, we can acknowledge our mistakes and ask our God Self for forgiveness. If we are truly sorry, through grace we are forgiven, and the negative karma is completely deleted from our life pattern.

All of God's laws work in a perfect way. Just as the Law of Grace and the Law of Karma are absolutely fair, so, too, is the process of reincarnation. We go from the physical to the astral to the celestial dimension in an orderly manner, leaving each dimension through the process called "death." So whether we are aware of it or not, all of us have experienced death many, many times. Yet each time we approach death, it seems so new that we often become fearful.

The fear of death seems to be a universal reaction. Perhaps we will not be completely free of our fear until we become enlightened. Our life experiences, personality, and religious beliefs are all important factors in determining the underlying causes of our fear and the strength of these emotions. It seems that one of the principal causes of the fear of death is our innate instinct for self-preservation. In this sense, fear is perfectly natural. It is unnatural only when it becomes an obstacle to life instead of protecting it.

Some may fear death because it is beyond their understanding and control. There is an instinctive fear of the unknown, and to most of us the World Beyond seems to be the unknown. Others may be apprehensive because they think that perhaps they have not lived as well as they should. Still others may fear death because they feel that they are too young to die. They don't want to die before they have truly experienced life. Some people try not to think about death and push such thoughts into the deepest recesses of their minds. Others view death as something that happens to someone else, but not to them. We may not merely fear the uncertainty of our own death; we may also fear losing someone we love.

The more we understand about death, the less likely we are to fear it. Just as birth marks the beginning of our new physical life, so death marks the end of our inhabiting a physical body. As we learn to deal positively with death, we will accept the fact that our life on Earth will one day end and we will cross through the doorway of death into a new life. Then we will realize that death isn't really as fearful as we had supposed.

As we age, the physical body goes through a natural deterioration — a chemical breakdown. No matter what we do, our physical body will not live forever. When it is time to cross into the next dimension through death, we discard our physical and energy (etheric) bodies. Then our Soul and consciousness take up residence in the emotional (astral) body, which closely resembles our physical body except that it vibrates at a much higher frequency. At death we leave behind us our material possessions and take with us all the accumulated knowledge, wisdom, and experiences that we have acquired during our sojourn on the Earth plane.

Natural death usually occurs gradually, especially in the case of the elderly and terminally ill. A gland emits a special hormone that slowly fills the bloodstream and is carried to every cell of the physical body in preparation for death. In the case of sudden death, this hormone is released instantly. As the bloodstream brings less and less oxygen, a numbness or natural anesthesia engulfs the dying brain. This may explain why many who have feared death accept it calmly when it finally comes.

Then comes the moment when the Soul is freed from the physical body. When the life cord is severed by the Angel of Death, we are dead to the physical world but alive in our new surroundings in the next dimension. When we are released from our physical body, a beloved friend, relative, or our Higher Self welcomes us and helps us to overcome any confusion or fear we may have experienced.

Those who have had a debilitating illness or who were mentally or physically handicapped before death are taken to a type of rest home where they will receive tender, loving care until they eventually realize that they are no longer encumbered by a physical body. My father broke his hip when he fell from a ladder while picking persimmons. He died soon after having a hip replacement. The first time I astrally visited him on the Other Side, he was in a beautiful nursing home that looked like an expensive resort. At first Dad was in a wheelchair, but when I visited him a few weeks he was up and walking. Soon he was ready to leave the nursing home and get on with his life in the World Beyond.

There are some people who, because of their religious beliefs, think that when you die you will sleep until "Gabriel blows his trumpet on Judgment Day." These people are taken to a dormitory-like area where they can sleep. Every once in awhile, a spirit worker comes through the wards blowing a trumpet and telling them that the time to awaken has arrived. Each time this happens, usually one or two will wake up from their sleep and begin their new life in the World Beyond.

Those who do not believe in life after death and

those who have experienced a sudden death may find their transition very confusing. Because the middle planes of the Astral World are so much like Earth, they often refuse to believe that they have died. Counselors patiently work with them until they finally understand that they are now alive in the World Beyond. Those who are enlightened spiritually are able to walk through the door of death without a loss of consciousness.

When people are emotionally ready, they will meet with their Higher Selves to review their recent life on Earth. With the guidance of spiritual counselors and the Higher Self, they begin the process of evaluating their past life. This evaluation is based on the intent of one's choices as much as on one's actions. Motivations are questioned but not condemned. If a lesson has not been learned, the Soul will be given another chance to learn it.

When we arrive in the Astral World, we are attracted to exactly the right place where we can continue our education and complete our work. We remain in the World Beyond as long as we have lessons to learn and work to finish, from a relatively short time to a hundred years or even longer. The farther along we are on our spiritual path, the less time we need to spend in the Astral World. Then, once again, we go through the process called "death." This time we leave behind our emotional (astral) body and take up residence in our soul body. This is our true Self — our Eternal Self.

Because the fifth dimension, or Celestial World, allows no negativity within its borders, it will be necessary for us to leave behind any negative karma that we may have brought with us. My Spiritual Teacher explains it this way: "Outside the gates of the Celestial World is a large waiting room. There are many lockers here with a name on each locker. If you have any negativity, you are to put it into your locker, where it will remain until you are ready to return to another physical life. Then once again, you will have the opportunity to take care of your negative karma and to learn the lessons that you have thus far failed to learn."

For those who are not spiritually evolved, the time spent in the Celestial World is like being in a deep sleep. They are unaware of the Higher Self's arms around them. They cannot appreciate the beauty, peace, and love that surrounds them. We who are more highly evolved are eager and excited to be once again united with our beloved Twin Soul, our Higher Self. We have come home.

Until enlightenment is attained, there will come a time, sooner or later, when a person is reminded that it is once again necessary to return to a physical life. While the peace and beauty of the higher dimensions may be hard to leave, we can also remember the physical and emotional pleasures of life in the physical world. The length of time between physical lives varies according to individual needs and choices. Some people who have died at a young age feel that they have missed the best part of their Earthly life and want to incarnate almost immediately. This happened with many of those who died during World War II. Even though their Higher Self suggested that they spend more time in the Astral World, they were anxious to return. Many of those who chose to be reborn almost immediately were the young men and women who were so opposed to the Vietnam War and had for their slogan, "Hell no, we won't go." They were opposed to war because they knew at first hand in their past life the devastation caused by war.

There are some who stubbornly resist coming into a physical body again. Even though their Higher Self explains why they need to incarnate, they are angry and come kicking and complaining into a new life. Some have incarnated many times as a male or female and they object to the suggestion that in this new lifetime they try life as the other sex. Some have experienced such emotionally or physically painful lives that they are fearful of returning to Earth. Eventually, with encouragement and instruction from their Higher Self, they begin to plan their new lives.

When the decision has been made to incarnate, a meeting is called of all those who are concerned with the progress of this particular Soul. Among those present are the person's guides, teachers, and Higher Self. They meet to discuss and plan the new life pattern with the incarnating Soul. Training sessions with spiritual counselors are provided to help prepare the Soul for a new life in the physical world.

During this time, past lives are reviewed and a chart is compiled showing all those qualities and lessons that the Soul still needs to experience. The decision is made whether to be male or female; also, the environment, nationality, and social and monetary status are chosen. Karmic assets and debts that were incurred in past lives are taken into consideration. The experiences and qualities that will help the person attain these goals are determined. This new life plan needs the approval of the Soul, who is guided in understanding that these experiences are necessary for further spiritual growth.

When the blueprint for the coming life has been completed, the information is fed into a spiritual *computer* which helps to determine the best parents for the incoming Soul. Then permission is obtained from the Higher Self of both the mother-to-be and father-to-be because there must be a mutual agreement between the future parents and the child who is drawn to them.

Groups of people tend to return to Earth together, so it may well be that the members of the chosen family will have been related in past lives. Because each child has a different reason for choosing us, it is not surprising that we do not feel the same toward all our children. Sometimes, because of a difference in temperament, parent and child seem to be on a collision course almost from the moment of birth. A parent may resent or feel estranged from a child who is radically different from the rest of the family. The parents may actually dislike their own child and, in turn, feel guilty because of these emotions. Parents need to remember that the child they love least is the one who needs love the most. Although we may not remember the past lives that we have shared, we can understand that each child has his own special reason for choosing us as their parents.

Because of the abuse they experienced as children, some may find it hard to believe that they chose their parents. We may not really understand why we made that choice, but we can be sure that there was a reason. Even if we are unsure of the negative karma that needs to be resolved between ourselves and our parents or children, unconditional love can heal all emotional wounds.

When the plans for the new life are completed, they are programmed into the life tapes of the incoming Soul. It is to be understood, however, that this future life is not planned down to the last detail: only a general outline is indicated. The more spiritually evolved we are, the less our life is preplanned. Of course, we all have free will and once we find ourselves in a physical body we have the choice whether or not to follow our blueprint. There are many who live their whole physical life and never remember what they came down to Earth to accomplish.

Now that all the decisions have been made, the incarnating Soul is gently placed into a *spiritual womb* awaiting the new birth. Many years ago, my Higher Self asked if I would like to see the spiritual womb where Souls are waiting to be born. I'm always interested in learning more about the higher dimensions, so I eagerly accepted the invitation. I was astrally taken to a large building that looked something like a laboratory. There I saw row after row of six-inch-square, open containers. There was a cone-shaped light a few inches above each one. Coming from these lights was a kaleidoscope of colors. I did not see anything inside these *cribs*, but I did feel a tremendous amount of love filling the whole place. My Higher Self told me that in each crib was a Soul waiting to be placed in a fetus and begin a new life on Earth. What a wonderful way to make the transition between the peace and joy of the higher dimension and the dualistic world of the physical plane!

An Angel of Birth determines when the time is right to bring the Soul from the spiritual womb and place it into the unborn fetus. This can occur at any time from conception to the moment of birth, but it usually occurs in the last trimester of the pregnancy. Until the Soul is united with the physical form, the fetus is not yet a human being. Once the fetus and Soul are joined, a new life is beginning.

Sometimes the Higher Self decides that something is physically wrong with the fetus or that the timing or family that has been selected is not right. If a miscarriage occurs before the fetus is ensouled, there is no death because there was no life. When a miscarriage occurs after the fetus is ensouled, the Soul is taken back to the spiritual womb to await another opportunity to incarnate. Sometimes the Soul returns to the same parents in another fetus at a later time. If the Higher Self determines, for some reason, to terminate the life *after* the baby is born, the Soul is taken to the Children's Heaven.

In the classes I teach in Parapsychology, most of my

students believe in reincarnation, but many say that this is their last incarnation on Earth. My reply is, "Good for you! This is the lifetime that you will take care of all your karmic debts, heal all your relationships, and walk the spiritual path of unconditional love. When you do this, you can attain enlightenment in this lifetime. Then you will no longer need to incarnate here on Earth. You will be able to learn and evolve in the higher realms. All of you have the potential to become Masters!"

The belief in reincarnation explains many of the seeming injustices experienced on Earth. It explains why one child is born into wealth and another born into poverty; why one child is born healthy and another born crippled or blind; why some are born with a higher degree of intelligence than others. We need to experience life as both a male and as a female. We need to learn how to handle poverty as well as great wealth. We draw certain problems and challenges into our life because we each have different lessons to learn and karmic debts to repay. To master all these lessons in one lifetime would be almost impossible. The cycle of birth and rebirth ends when we have learned the lessons of life and love and have achieved enlightenment.

12

Surviving in the 21st Century

In my sleep, I heard a rumbling noise that sounded like a truck coming right through the house. Then everything began to shake violently. Half asleep and half awake, I felt bricks falling on top of me, crushing me to death. When I opened my eyes and realized that I was safe in my own bed, I understood that I must be reliving a past life in Atlantis when a brick wall had crushed me to death during a terrifying earthquake. As my consciousness adjusted to the present, I heard my son, Dale, yell from his bedroom, "Is anyone alive in there?" Thank God, all four of my children were unhurt, but my son Mark had missed injury or death by only a couple of inches when a heavy window air conditioner fell onto his bed. Our house was knocked off its foundation and the walls were cracked. The large aquarium in the living room had broken, and goldfish were flopping around on the wet carpet. In the kitchen, broken glass and food from the refrigerator were ankle deep. Everything was a mess — but all of us had survived the killer San Fernando earthquake.

Concerned that the children in my class at Gridley Elementary would soon be arriving at school, I got dressed and drove toward San Fernando, where I was teaching at the time. The farther I drove, the more damage was apparent. Finally the roads in front of me were blocked off by the police, and only emergency vehicles were being allowed through. My only option was to turn around and go home.

A short while after I got home, the police drove

down our street, announcing over a loudspeaker that we had half an hour to evacuate our homes and leave the area. Later we learned that the dam above us had cracked and was on the verge of breaking. Had this happened, the whole area would have been flooded. My children and I hurriedly packed a few clothes. We couldn't find our frightened cat and had to leave without her. We were more fortunate than most of the people who were evacuated that day, because my mother and dad lived ten miles away in Van Nuys, where only minor damage had occurred. For the next week, my folks shared their home with us.

The first time I saw my classroom after the earthquake, I could hardly believe the damage that had occurred. There were large cracks in the walls and ceiling, and the concrete floor had buckled. The furniture had been thrown about, and all the light fixtures had pulled loose and lay on the floor. The desks bore deep scars from the falling light fixtures, but the children had even deeper emotional scars as a result of the trauma of the earthquake and the death of two of our students. If the earthquake had occurred three hours later when the children were in class, there would have been a great number of casualties, because our school was near the epicenter.

If you ever have to evacuate from your home, planning ahead will help you think more clearly in a time of great confusion and stress. Whether your home is exposed to the danger of a wildfire sweeping down the mountainside, or a river overflowing its banks and lapping at your front door, or a hurricane, it is wise to be prepared to leave at a moment's notice. If you have only a few minutes' warning, you need to have your priorities clearly in mind. Keep all important papers in an easy-to-carry container in an accessible place. Pack your car with fruit, snacks, water, pillows, blankets, flashlights, and any necessary medication. Most important of all, don't forget your credit cards, checkbook, and cash.

Even though you may never have to be evacuated, you may still need to be self-sufficient when disaster strikes. I live in the country now, and when high winds blow trees onto the power lines, our electricity is sometimes off for several days. When I lose electrical power, I begin to realize how much I depend on it. I have found that it's wise to have several different sources of light: candles, lanterns, oil lamps, and flashlights. For heat, I have a wood stove and lots of wood. I also have an ample supply of canned food and a manual can-opener, since it's difficult to cook frozen or dried food over a wood stove. The electricity runs the well pump, too, so I store water in plastic containers and refill them often to keep the water fresh. To keep informed about the current situation, a battery-powered radio is essential.

When survivors of an earthquake, fire, tornado, hurricane, or flood are interviewed on television, they often express their thanks to God that their family is alive. Usually their experience dramatically changes their priorities. Although the survivors may have lost everything except the clothes on their backs, they realize that material possessions aren't as important as they once thought, compared to the lives of their loved ones.

It would seem that we are experiencing an ever-increasing number of natural catastrophes and severe weather patterns. What is happening now is a prelude to what we can expect in the next few years. The most powerful and devastating weather conditions of the 20th century were caused by the warming of the Pacific Ocean. This El Niño effect in 1997 and 1998 caused damage that has been estimated to exceed $33 billion worldwide, and this does not even take into consideration the human toll of the accompanying floods, droughts, famines, and wildfires. El Niño turned typical weather patterns upside down, drying the lush rain forests and turning arid plains into wetlands. Scientists agree that El Niño cycles have become more frequent and progressively warmer over the past century. The cooler La Niña generally exaggerates weather conditions that are considered normal. One of the results of this cooling trend is that hurricanes in the Atlantic gather more strength as they move westward. The 1998 La Niña hurricane season was the deadliest in the past two centuries. It is believed that the effect of future El Niños and La Niñas on the weather will continue to intensify for the next few decades.

Several of my friends have asked me where they should move to escape the impending catastrophes. My answer is, "Do not move out of fear, but be guided by your Higher Self. Wherever you are and whatever happens to you will be exactly what you need to experience." As enlightened beings, we know that we are eternal; therefore, we have no fear of the future. We know that when we ask, our Higher Self will guide and protect us. Nothing can happen to us that is not a part of our life plan. Enlightenment helps take away our fear and gives us strength and wisdom to face the future with confidence.

There are some who believe that the increase in natural catastrophes indicates that we are approaching the end of the world. It all depends on which world we are talking about. To be sure, the world of greed, hatred, and negativity is coming to an end. Apocalyptic predictions relate that we are approaching a final cataclysm which will destroy the power of evil and usher in the kingdom of God. Each time a civilization has allowed negativity and greed to flourish, destruction has come to put an end to the imbalance. Both the flood in Noah's time and the sinking of

Atlantis are examples of this. As we prepare to enter the new age, Earth is going to experience a period of cleansing which will help to wipe out the negativity that has caused us so many problems in the past.

Even two thousand years ago, people were concerned about the end of the age. When Jesus' disciples asked him about this, he said, "When I return the world will be as indifferent to the things of God as the people were in Noah's day. They ate and drank and married, everything just as usual, right up to the day when Noah went into the ark and the flood came and destroyed them all" (Luke 17:26-27).

"When you hear of wars and insurrections, don't panic. True, wars must come, but the end of the age won't follow immediately, for nation shall rise against nation and kingdom against kingdom. There will be great earthquakes, and famines in many lands, and epidemics, and terrifying things happening in the heavens" (Luke 21:9-11).

"The courage of many people will falter because of the fearful fate they see coming upon the Earth, for the stability of the very heavens will be broken up. Then the peoples of Earth shall see me, the Messiah, coming in a cloud with power and great glory. So when all these things begin to happen, stand straight and look up for your salvation is near" (Luke 21:26-28; *Living Bible*, paraphrased).

It's significant that Jesus referred to Noah and the great flood as one of the signs of the coming age. Legends of a great flood are common to almost all peoples. Besides the memory of a worldwide flood, there are also myths of recurring catastrophes that almost wiped out mankind, leaving only a few survivors. These stories are so prevalent and widespread that they seem almost to be race memories. They tell of changes in the surface of the Earth caused by cataclysms such as volcanic explosions and violent earthquakes that pushed up mountains while other land masses sank beneath the sea. All these great catastrophes may be linked to the movement of the Earth's crust.

The Earth's crust varies in thickness from about five miles under the oceans to about twenty miles under the continents. One theory that scientists have developed is that the crust consists of about twenty rigid plates that are in continuous slow motion. Most of the world's earthquakes and active volcanoes occur where these plates slide past or collide with one another. A polar shift could occur when there is a sudden violent movement of the Earth's crust.

It is believed that Earth has been rotating on its present axis for about seven thousand years. At that time, the magnetic poles moved away from the axial poles. The shifting of Earth's crust would result in new positions of the North and South poles and would probably set in motion a long period of volcanic eruptions, earthquakes, and climate changes which could include a new ice age. The former polar ice caps would melt because of the higher temperatures, while new icecaps or glaciers would form where once the climate had been warmer.

Scientists believe that there have been at least four major ice ages since the beginning of planet Earth. There is evidence to prove that the Arctic and Antarctic were once warm, and that the Sahara Desert was once a sea. Fossil mollusks and seashells found in the Himalayas, the highest mountains in the world, indicate that they were at one time under water.

The last polar shift may have occurred in the time of Noah. The cause of the great flood was probably not just rain falling on the land. A polar shift, combined with earthquakes, tsunami waves, and melting icecaps could have raised the water level thousands of feet, creating a worldwide flood. An earlier polar shift may have caused the sinking of Atlantis and, still earlier, the sinking of Lemuria.

What force could possibly be so powerful that it could jolt Earth's crust hard enough to cause it to slip suddenly into a new position? There may be several circumstances that could trigger a polar shift. One may have occurred when a giant meteor or comet smashed into the Gulf of Mexico off the Yucatán Peninsula. Another may have been when Meldek, the fifth planet of our solar system, was destroyed, causing the gravitational balance of Earth to be temporarily thrown off. At that time, the Earth's axis may have moved several degrees from its former position.

In the future, when our solar system moves into the Photon Belt, this powerful electromagnetic energy may cause an increase in stress which could build up the breaking point, causing another change in the geographical positions of Earth's axial and magnetic poles.

When Earth, along with the rest of our solar system, enters the Photon Belt, every living thing will be affected. Earth will never again be the same after the vibrations are raised to the fourth dimension. Because of the magnitude of the Photon Belt, we are already feeling some of its effects. The actual time when the solar system is completely engulfed by this electromagnetic energy has yet to be revealed, but many believe it will be before the year 2012. Those who have not prepared themselves for Earth's changes will not be able to survive for long in this higher energy field. If we are to survive, it will be necessary for us to raise our vibrations, through love, so that we can withstand this tremendous electromagnetic energy. It is important that we are physically, emotionally, and mentally prepared for this extraordinary event.

Some of the Higher Beings have said that there may

be three days of darkness when we fully enter the Photon Belt. This darkness may be caused by a series of volcanic eruptions that will send ash and debris into the atmosphere. It might also be caused by a comet or an asteroid crashing into Earth, which could create a cloud of dust and debris that would block the light of the Sun for months. If some morning we wake up and there is only darkness, we should not panic. It has been suggested that we stay in or near our homes during this period of darkness, because there may be mass hysteria among those who are unaware. In some respects, the darkness will act as a wake-up call. It will certainly get people's attention, and they will begin to realize that something monumental is taking place.

We can't create a bright new Earth if we keep doing things the same old way. The time for Earth's transformation is now. All around us, everything is moving and changing. We may find ourselves wondering just what is going on and what is the purpose of all this. These changes are absolutely necessary if the vibrations of Earth and her inhabitants are to be raised to the fourth dimension. We need to be open and not resist these changes. Now is the time for Earth to be transformed into a fourth-dimensional planet. Then Earth will no longer be surrounded by the negativity which she has endured for countless ages, and the dualistic nature of the physical world will no longer be felt.

We may not be able to comprehend how Earth's transformation will take place, but we can trust that what we truly need to know will be revealed to us. In this way, we can experience an inner peace and centeredness. We should be excited about what is happening to our planet. It is certainly wise to be prepared for this transformation, but we do not need to dwell upon the impending changes or fear the future. We can learn to focus our attention on the present moment and trust that all is going according to a greater cosmic plan. Any preoccupation we may have concerning our survival will begin to fade away, and feelings of helplessness or fear will be gone. The end of the world is not imminent, because the world of light and love cannot be destroyed. Now more than in any other time in Earth's history, enlightenment is important because it enables us to change our perspective about the future from one of doom and gloom to one of faith and anticipation of a bright new world.

As we enter the 21st century, we have several options. Many of us have chosen to be survivors and remain on Earth to be of service to those who are searching for answers and inner peace. Some have chosen to be physically beamed aboard a spacecraft where they will be prepared to return to Earth at a later time. Others have chosen to leave Earth, through death, and continue their work in the Higher Realms. Those who have failed to raise their vibrations through love will be sent to another planet when they die. There they will continue their education until they too become enlightened. Then the lower planes of the Astral World will cease to exist, because they will no longer be needed.

In our orderly world we have natural cycles: a day, the time it takes the Earth to rotate on its axis; a year, the time it takes Earth to circle the Sun; a millennium, a thousand years; an age, which is a little over two thousand years; and a polar day, which is about twenty-five thousand years.

In ancient Assyria, priests discovered a band of stars that appear to encircle the Earth. They divided these star groups or constellations into twelve parts which became the twelve signs of the Zodiac. Ancient astronomers observed the changing position of these constellations through which the Sun appears to move over the course of a year. They also discovered that the time it takes for Earth to move through one sign of the Zodiac is a little more than two thousand years, the length of an age. It takes Earth about twenty-five thousand years to move through all twelve signs of the Zodiac, which has been referred to as a polar day.

Earth is now moving out of the Piscean and into the Aquarian Age. The name Aquarius means "water carrier," and its symbol comes from the Egyptian hieroglyph for "running water." Astrologers believe that the various signs of the Zodiac not only influence the lives of people but also Earth itself. Many of the characteristics of people born under the sign of Aquarius may also be reflected in Earth as we move into the new age. These characteristics include unpredictability, unexpected change, and a curiosity which makes it possible to invent new ways of doing things. Aquarians usually have quite advanced ideas and may become impatient with those who continue to do things in the same old way. They tend to be intuitive, philosophical, and interested in the mystical things of life. Aquarians also have a great love of freedom and liberty. These characteristics are certainly appropriate for Earth in the coming age.

Everything we have done in our lives up to this moment is exactly what we needed to do. Every experience has been essential for our spiritual growth, or else we would not have needed to experience it. We are quite literally creating our future by what we are thinking at this very moment.

Now is the time for each one of us to claim our spiritual birthright. There are some who seem to be sleeping, unaware of the real reason why they are here on Earth. While it is true that we are all spiritual Beings, some have forgotten their divinity. This prevents them from claiming their natural birthright. These people will continue to work toward spiritual enlightenment from life to life until they achieve their Mastership. It's time for us to wake up! When we are truly awake, we will let go of our sense of separateness and realize that we are one with our God Self. Our minds will be opened to the higher consciousness and we will know that we are eternal Beings with unlimited potential. Because of the energies that are pouring into Earth at this time, more and more people will awaken to the realization that they can achieve enlightenment in this lifetime.

If enlightenment is the key to our survival, how then do we achieve it? Simply because our vibrations are raised to a higher dimension doesn't mean that we suddenly become enlightened. Whatever unlearned lessons and unresolved relationships we have in the third dimension, we will take with us wherever we go. There we will once again be given the opportunity to learn these lessons and resolve all our relationships.

If we accept the fact that we have within us everything that it takes to be enlightened and that the Truth is always available to us through our Higher Self, we will not need to look for someone to *enlighten* us. We will not need to search for a teacher or guru who has the answers. The fact is that in the physical world there are no perfect gurus or teachers. We should not surrender our free will to any authority figure or rely completely on one. Instead, we need to trust our own intuition.

Every one of us has the right to choose our own personal spiritual path. At the same time, we do not need to be concerned about the path that someone else has chosen. We are not here to save others — only ourselves. Religions have different names for enlightenment. Whatever the name, it is concerned with the highest state of awareness. There are many paths which lead to enlightenment, and we need discernment to choose the right path for us. Each of us has our own truth, our own belief system. There is also cosmic Truth, God's unchanging, everlasting Truth. When our truth and God's Truth are one and the same, we will have achieved our goal: we will be enlightened.

Love is the perfect path to enlightenment, and it is available to every one of us. When we raise our vibrations through love, we will find life growing more wondrous every day. Vibrations are the actual substance of existence. We become the vibration which we create with our thoughts and emotions. Therefore, we can control our vibrations by controlling our thoughts and emotions. As we become filled with love, our vibrations will be raised higher and higher. Within the cells of our body, the light particles will begin to vibrate more rapidly. This incredible vibration of love will awaken every cell of the body, and each molecule will become filled with light and love. The perfect path to enlightenment is unconditional, nonjudgmental love.

Each of us has been endowed by God with the gift of free will. That means that we are in control of our own lives, and not just puppets who react when a string is pulled. As enlightened Beings, we need to recognize the responsibility of free will. It is up to us if we use our free will in a positive or negative way. Other people also have a right to use their free will as they desire. We are not to judge anyone for the choices they make. Giving others the freedom to be themselves is one of the most important lessons to learn — and perhaps the hardest. Each of us is responsible for his or her own choices. If we choose to do God's will, we can reach our full potential and become enlightened in this lifetime.

Becoming enlightened doesn't mean that we will never again be faced with problems. It does mean that we can change our problems into learning experiences. It also means that we can be centered and at peace in the midst of difficulty. We may find ourselves dealing with doubts and fears. Although we usually try to do our very best, we may become discouraged because we feel that we have fallen short of our goal of perfection. We live in an imperfect world, and even a Master who incarnates in a physical body may find it difficult to follow a perfect path. We need to rise above any doubts that we may have and not let our faults or failures be a reason for giving up our goal of achieving enlightenment.

Even when we do achieve enlightenment, we may find that some choices are so complicated and some temptations so strong that we may do something in a moment of weakness or selfishness that we know is wrong. When we have said or done something which we regret, we can ask to be forgiven. Through grace, our Higher Self not only forgives, but also forgets so that we have no karmic debt to repay. We need to accept this forgiveness and love ourselves unconditionally even when we feel that we are not perfect or are not living up to our full potential.

When we finally realize that we are far more important than we have even dared to dream, we will never again have any need to inflate our egos with imagined importance. Those who think that they have more knowledge than others or feel that they are closer to becoming enlightened have a greater responsibility precisely because of this. Some who are already Masters have fallen into an ego trap of needing to tell others who they are. If you are a Master, you do not need to tell anyone. The time will come when your true identity will be easily recognized. We should not feel superior to others *because we're not*. The truth is that we are all equal. Only when we realize this will we begin to see ourselves as being a part of a universe of equal

Beings all equally essential to the whole.

It is time to recognize who we really are and why we are on the Earth plane at this time. We need to remember that many of us volunteered to help Earth and her inhabitants transcend the third-dimensional consciousness. We are preparing to enter a new age where there will be restored ecological balance, international cooperation, and universal harmony. All of us will be working together to achieve the full potential of our beautiful planet. All races and religions will come together with a single spiritual consciousness. Their goal will be brotherhood and unity of all the inhabitants of Earth. We should have an attitude of expectancy as we prepare for this new age that will bring, peace, love, and harmony to planet Earth.

As Masters, we will know who we are and why we chose to incarnate in the physical world. As we understand the true purpose of our life on Earth, it will all begin to make sense. Self-doubt will be replaced with a sense of serenity, joy, and contentment. We will understand how to turn our dreams and aspirations into the reality we desire. We will no longer fear death because we know where we are going. We also know that infinite possibilities lie ahead of us in the Higher Realms.

As we achieve enlightenment, people around us will begin to notice not only a physical but also an emotional change in us. We may appear to be younger and more full of life than others our age. People will see a glow around us as we become filled with optimism and enthusiasm for the adventure of life. Those who need our help will feel our love and empathy and will be drawn to us like a magnet. We will experience the joy and satisfaction of helping others.

We will begin to notice changes in ourselves. We will discover that we are becoming more patient and overflowing with love. We will begin to replace any resentment with tolerance, and we will stop judging others. We will find that we are listening more closely to our body, which has always been giving us signals whenever we are fatigued or stressed or ill. We will realize how unique we are, and we won't compare ourselves to anyone else. Nor will we need anyone's approval for our actions. We will know that, with our Higher Self, we are a complete person who lacks for nothing. We will create our own Heaven here on Earth. We won't have to go anywhere to find it, because we know that Heaven is not a place but the realization of the fact that we are one with God.

Eventually the time will come when we are to leave the physical world. Now that we have achieved enlightenment, we may wonder how this will be different from the other times we have been with our Higher Self in the Celestial World. We may also wonder why we have been unable to remember these experiences. The reason is that each time we have been born into a physical body, a veil has covered our minds, causing us to forget. If it were not for this, we would be so homesick for our beloved Higher Self that we would not be able to accomplish the work we have chosen to do.

As ascended Masters, we will no longer need to return to Earth in a physical body. We will be completely free of Earth and its karma. We will also be free of the astral world and it will no longer be necessary for us to spend time there. When we ascend into the Celestial World, we will be united with our Higher Self. Some believe that there will be a melding and the two will become one Being. Others believe that we will be together as two complementary parts which together make a whole. Whichever is true, we will experience the joy and peace of being united with our beloved Higher Self.

We will have the wonderful opportunity to learn, grow, and be of service to others. It takes humility to truly be of service. The Great Masters are always humble. Humility does not mean a lack of self-love or self-esteem. Rather it is the willingness to be of service to others without seeking recognition for our contribution and help.

Some of us may choose to return to the physical or astral world as teachers and Avatars. Some may choose to remain in the Celestial World with their Higher Self where they can enjoy a much-needed vacation in an environment of peace, harmony, and love. Whichever choice we make will be for the glory of God. As ascended Masters, we will discover that our greatest joy is in assisting others in their spiritual quest. Glorious opportunities await us when we have finally achieved enlightenment.

Glossary

Acupressure: alternative healing; uses pressure instead of needles on acupoints.

Acupuncture: thin needles inserted into specific parts of body for healing and pain relief.

Affirmation: a short, positive statement.

Alpha brain waves: occurs during meditation, light sleep; 8 to 13 cycles per second.

Alpha state: altered state of consciousness achieved during meditation, light sleep; necessary for all psychic experiences.

Alternative healing: differs from Western medicine by tapping into the body's natural defense system.

Amnesia: inability to retrieve memories.

Androgynous: expressing as both male and female.

Archangels: created Beings who are higher and more advanced than the rank of angels.

Ascended Master: a Master who has left the physical world and dwells in the Higher Realms.

Astral body: another name for emotional body; primary body used in the Astral World.

Astral World: World Beyond; vibrates at a faster rate; interpenetrates the physical world.

Aura: color-filled portion of astral body which extends past the physical body; emotions and health affect colors.

Avatar: a master who returns to Earth as a spiritual teacher and leader.

Beta brain waves: waking consciousness; 13 to 40 cycles per second.

Biofeedback therapy: method of monitoring and eventually controlling physiological responses by using an electroencephalograph.

Biorhythm: fluctuation of body energy and emotions during day, week, or month.

Brow center: located between eyebrows; linked to pineal gland; activates clairvoyance; violet ray.

Celestial Realm: above Astral World; dwelling place of Higher Self, Masters, and Archangels.

Centers: seven energy vortexes in the etheric body; also called chakras.

Chakras: another name for centers; wheels of energy.

Chiropractic medicine: healing by manipulation and adjustments to body.

Clairaudience: the ability to hear sounds beyond normal range of hearing by using the sixth sense; ESP.

Clairvoyance: the ability to see or know things that are beyond normal vision by using the sixth sense; ESP.

Conscious mind: concerned with rational, logical, conceptual thought.

Cosmic consciousness: enlightenment; aware of cosmic Truth.

Cosmic justice: absolute, perfect justice.

Cosmic Lords: great Archangels; first created Beings.

Cosmic Truth: absolute Truth.

Crown center: top of head; linked with pituitary gland; connection to Higher Self; pure white ray.

Déja vu: the feeling of already having experienced or seen something before.

Delta brain waves: deep sleep; 4 to 7 cycles per second.

Electroencephalogram: EEG; record of brain waves.

Emotional biorhythm: 28-day cycle; results in emotional ups and downs.

Emotional body: another name for the astral body; primary body used in the Astral World; several inches larger than physical body and interpenetrates it.

Energy body: also called etheric body; inch larger than physical body; interpenetrates and energizes physical body.

Enlightenment: cosmic consciousness; spiritual insight.

Eternal Now: timelessness in the Higher Realms.

Etheric body: another name for energy body; interpenetrates physical body.

Extrasensory perception: ESP; sixth sense; ability to see, feel, hear, and in some cases, smell and taste in Astral World.

Extraterrestrials: beings not originating on Earth.

False memories: remembering something that never really happened.

Fifth dimension: Celestial realms; dwelling place of Higher Self, Masters, Archangels.

Fourth dimension: present Astral World; interpenetrates third dimension; invisible to physical eyes because of higher vibrations.

Functional mental illness: no apparent physical brain damage yet mind does not work properly.

Grace: spiritual form of forgiveness.

Guardian Angel: also known as Twin Soul, Higher Self, Oversoul, God Self.

Heart center: superimposes thymus; bridge between

physical and spiritual centers; green ray.

Higher Beings: Masters, Angels, Archangels, Planetary, Solar, Cosmic, and Universal Lords.

Higher Realms: fifth dimension and above.

Higher Self: Twin Soul; the part of a human that is perfect; the human and Higher Self are one yet they express as two beings; Guardian Angel.

Homeopathic therapy: uses small doses of herbs, etc., in extremely diluted solution for healing.

Intuition: knowing something without conscious reasoning; information from Higher Self.

Karma: law of cause and effect; every thought, word, deed influences our life.

Kirlian photography: method of taking pictures of the electromagnetic field emanating from astral body of plants and humans.

Kundalini: life force or prana traveling upward through all seven etheric centers.

Left hemisphere: part of brain that deals with rational, logical thought.

Massage therapy: releases muscle tension; promotes healing.

Master: person who has learned all lessons, cleared all karma, and does not need to return to a physical body.

Mastership: the proficiency and authority of a Master.

Meditation: quieting conscious mind and tuning into Higher Self, alpha state.

Mental biorhythm: cycle of 33 days; causes variation in mental ability.

Meridians: major pathways for life energy to flow through body.

Naturopathy: method of healing using natural ways, including herbal remedies.

Navel center: superimposes pancreas gland; connecting point between energy and physical bodies; orange ray.

Neurotransmitters: chemicals in brain, too little or too much may result in mental disorders.

Optimism: anticipating the best possible outcome for any action or happening.

Organic mental illness: results from birth defect; illness or injury causing brain damage.

Pessimism: expecting the worst outcome for any action or happening.

Phobias: dread or intense fear of a particular situation or object.

Photon Belt: huge mass of light and electromagnetic energy which will affect our solar system.

Physical biorhythm: 23-day cycle; causes variation in energy.

Pineal gland: located near center of brain; considered the third eye and inner ear of astral body.

Planetary Lords: Archangels in charge of the various planets in the universe.

Prana: life force or energy; vitality.

Prayer: communication with Higher Self.

Prime Creator: God Almighty.

Reflexology: healing method; pressure applied to specific places on foot corresponding to particular body location.

Reincarnation: belief that the Soul is immortal and only returns in a human body.

REM sleep: rapid eye movement during dreaming.

Renegades: negative extraterrestrials; outcasts sent to Earth from other planets.

Right hemisphere: part of brain that is creative and intuitive.

Sexual center: also called root center; superimposes reproductive glands; red ray.

Solar Lords: Archangels in charge of the various solar systems in the universes.

Solar plexus center: connecting point between emotional and physical bodies; superimposes adrenal gland; yellow ray.

Soul body: extends past the astral body and interpenetrates the physical, energy, and emotional body; primary body above Astral World; eternal.

Soul mate: someone we have loved in many lives, as parent and child, as siblings, as lovers; may meet none or several soul mates in one lifetime.

Spiritual body: another name for soul body; primary body above Astral World.

Spiritual path: way to enlightenment; path of unconditional, nonjudgmental love.

Spiritual womb: a waiting place for Souls before they are placed into a fetus.

Subconscious mind: records thoughts and emotions and stores them as memories.

Superconscious mind: telepathic connection between

human and Higher Self.

Telepathy: communication between one mind and another by using the sixth sense; thought transference.

Third dimension: present physical world in which we live.

Thought form: psychic form created by the mind; can be positive or negative.

Throat center: superimposes thyroid gland; activates clairaudience; blue ray.

Transmigration: belief that the Soul is immortal and can return in an animal or human body.

Twin Soul: Higher Self; Twin Flame; Guardian Angel.

Unconscious mind: autonomic nervous system.

Universal Lords: Archangels in charge of the universes; Creator Lords.

Visualization: ability to create mental pictures in the mind; can be positive or negative.

Voodoo: can be used to create negative thought form or cast an evil spell.

White light: God essence flowing from God through Higher Self to us; power to heal and protect.

World Beyond: another name for the Astral World.

Further Reading

Exploring the World Beyond: A True Astral Adventure is the companion to this book. Accompany a class of college students as they astrally visit a land that is not far from here but is invisible to our eyes and shrouded in mystery. Most of the people who go there are not heard from again, yet it is the place where we will reside when we leave our physical bodies through death. Some refer to this place as the Astral World, Heaven, or Hell, or the World Beyond. Each chapter contains exciting information about our future home. The valuable teachings and insights of the author will help to unveil many of the mysteries that surround the World Beyond.

Both *Exploring the World Beyond* and additional copies of *Enlightenment: The Key to Survival in the 21st Century* are available at your local bookstore or may be ordered from:

BookPartners, Inc.
P.O. Box 922
Wilsonville, Oregon 97070

Phone: (503) 682-9821
Order: 1-800-895-7323
Fax: (503) 682-8684
E-mail: bpbooks@teleport.com

Book: $14.95   Shipping/Handling: $3.50
for each additional book: $2.00

About the Author

FranCelia Woodward received her degree in Psychology from Pepperdine University. She made the transition to parapsychology after the life-changing experience which she writes about in the Preface of *Exploring the World Beyond*, the companion volume to *Enlightenment*.

After teaching thirty years for the Los Angeles Board of Education, Mrs. Woodward retired, but she has continued to teach classes in parapsychology. Mrs. Woodward has three sons and a daughter, as well as six grandchildren.

The author is clairvoyant and clairaudient and has touched many lives through her classes and counseling. She is the Northwest director of The Inner Voice, a non-profit organization dedicated to helping people discover their innate abilities. Other books she has authored include *Numerology: Key to Relationships*; *Extraterrestrials*; and *Steps to Ascension*.

If you would like information about these books or would like to learn how to receive personal counseling, please send a stamped, self-addressed envelope to:

FranCelia Woodward
c/o The Inner Voice
84980 Chezem Road
Eugene, OR 97405